FRAY ANGÉLICO CHÁVEZ

Pasó Por Aquí
Series on the Nuevomexicano Literary Heritage
Edited by Genaro M. Padilla,
Erlinda Gonzales-Berry, and A. Gabriel Meléndez

Frontispiece Fray Angélico Chávez, Burros
(courtesy of the Franciscan Archives, Cincinnati)

FRAY ANGÉLICO CHÁVEZ

Poet, Priest, and Artist

Edited by
ELLEN McCRACKEN

University of New Mexico Press
Albuquerque

Pasó Por Aquí
Series on the Nuevomexicano Literary Heritage
Edited by Genaro M. Padilla,
Erlinda Gonzales-Berry, and
A. Gabriel Meléndez

Library of Congress
Cataloging-in-Publication Data
Fray Angélico Chávez : poet, priest, and artist /
edited by Ellen McCracken. — 1st ed.
p.   cm. — (Pasó por aquí)
Includes bibliographical references and index.
ISBN 0-8263-2007-4 (alk. paper).
1. Chávez, Angélico, 1910—Criticism and interpretation.
2. Christianity and literature—New Mexico—History—20th century.
3. Christianity and art—New Mexico—History—20th century.
4. Christian poetry, American—History and criticism.
5. New Mexico—Historiography.
6. New Mexico—In literature.
I. McCracken, Ellen.
II. Series.
PS3505.H625   Z66   2000
818'.5209—dc21
99-050726

CONTENTS

III The Life of a Franciscan

NOTE FROM THE SERIES EDITOR

It is indeed fitting that this collection of essays on the lifelong work of Fray Angélico Chávez be included in the *Pasó Por Aquí Series*, a series dedicated to the recovery of the Nuevomexicano literary tradition and to honoring exceptional Nuevomexicanos who have contributed to that tradition. No more exceptional an individual than Fray Angélico Chávez is to be found in the history of the cultural production by New Mexico's hijos nativos.

At the tender age of fourteen, Angélico Chávez left New Mexico to join a seminary in Cincinnati, Ohio. One cannot help but wonder whether it was nostalgia for family and homeland that nourished the gifted imagination of this young man. At any rate, his exuberant creative spirit soon gave way to writing verse and drama, to painting, and to drawing. As his studies progressed, he developed a strong interest in history, which would, in subsequent years, make him one of the most prolific contributors to New Mexican historiography. His adolescent dabbling in creative literature would likewise blossom into an impressive body of literary work that reveals his profound love for his homeland and its people. His cultural production and intellectual pursuits, however, did not end here. Painting, genealogy, philology, and biography are but a few of the creative and scholarly genres he fashioned, leaving an oeuvre the quality and breadth of which truly define him as a renaissance scholar.

The editor of this book observes, "the twenty-three books and over six hundred other pieces merely scratches the surface of his extraordinary contributions to twentieth-century American letters." Yet, despite this prolific body of work, Fray Angélico has not received the attention he deserves from scholars. Ellen McCracken is to be commended for having had the foresight to take this crucial first step toward acknowledging the extraordinary breadth and importance of Fray Angélico's work and for setting the foundation for continued scholarly assessment of his contributions, not only to New Mexican but to American historiography, arts, and letters.

Erlinda Gonzales-Berry
Gabriel Meléndez
Genaro Padilla

General Editors
Pasó Por Aquí Series

ACKNOWLEDGMENTS

I wish to thank the nine other contributors to this volume for their timely response to my request for essays on Fray Angélico Chávez, their innovative and meticulous research, and their enthusiasm for the work of this great New Mexico humanist. It has been a privilege to work with each one of the authors who individually and jointly have made possible a multi-voiced book.

Underlying this collective publication is an even larger group of individuals and institutions whose support has been crucial to the project. UC MEXUS, under the direction of Juan-Vicente Palerm, provided both a research grant and a small grant that aided in the publication of this book. The University of California, Santa Barbara, provided sabbatical leave, a Regents' Humanities Faculty Fellowship, and research grants from the Academic Senate and the Interdisciplinary Humanities Center that made possible the research, writing, and editing involved in this book.

I thank Elizabeth Hadas, Andrea Otañez, and Barbara Guth of the University of New Mexico Press for their support of this project throughout the long process of publication. I am grateful to the Editorial Board of the press and the outside reader for the helpful suggestions offered, and to Erlinda Gonzales-Berry and Genaro Padilla, editors of the *Pasó Por Aquí* Series. Judy Sacks carefully copyedited the entire manuscript, a daunting task when ten authors are involved. Mario García, John Kessell, and Father Thomas Steele, S.J. read and provided comments on several of the essays. Laura Weingarten, Gabriela Sánchez, and Magdalena Torres provided valuable research assistance in retrieving Fray Angélico's numerous publications. I am especially indebted to Phyllis Morgan (Morales) for her carefully prepared bibliography of Fray Angélico's writings to 1978, without which the difficult task of collecting his hundreds of publications would have been nearly impossible.

For granting permission to reprint photographs and quotations, I wish to thank Father Dan Anderson, O.F.M.; Tom Chávez; Father Jeremy Harrington, O.F.M.; John Kessell; and Marina Ochoa.

A number of people took time from their busy schedules to provide material or grant interviews for the biography of Fray Angélico that I am writing with Mario García. The information they provided had a great impact on the introduction, my essay in this volume, and the editing of the book as a whole. At the Fray Angélico Chávez History Library and Photographic Archives at the Palace of the Governors in Santa Fe, Orlando Romero and Tom Chávez patiently provided extensive research material and insight into the life and work of Fray Angélico. They kindly allowed extra research hours and went out of their way to help, as did Charles Bennett, Hazel Romero, Arthur Olivas, Richard Rudisill, Diana Ortega De Santis, and, more recently, the new director of the library, Tomas Jaehn. Marina Ochoa, head of the archives of the Archdiocese of Santa Fe, made available key historical documents and offered important information about Fray Angélico's contribution to the archives and the cathedral renovations. Father Virgilio Biasiol, O.F.M., director of the Santa Barbara Mission Archive-Library, allowed me to do extensive research and photocopying of material from the archives' rich collection of Franciscan documents and publications.

I am grateful to Father Dan Anderson, O.F.M., archivist of the Franciscan Archives of St. John the Baptist Province in Cincinnati, for his generosity and professional acumen in facilitating my research on Fray Angélico, especially the time he took to have many of the photographs in this book reproduced. He and the other members of the Pleasant Street Friary—Fathers Jack Wintz, Murray Bodo, and Jovian Weigel, who opened their home to me in 1997 and provided many insights into the life of Fray Angélico—are models of the dynamic Franciscanism that continues to make its mark as we enter the new millennium. Father Marcan Hetteberg and Brother Dan Rewers provided valuable research assistance and good company during the long hours in the archives.

For offering their time and insight by granting interviews or providing written testimonies about their remembrances of Fray Angélico Chávez, I wish to thank: Rudolfo Anaya; Father Salvador Aragón, O.F.M.; Carlota Baca; Alice Ann Biggerstaff; Father Godfrey Blank, O.F.M.; Tim Burch; Father Crispin Butz, O.F.M.; Consuelo Chávez; Teresa Chávez; José Cisneros; Saul Cohen; María Dean; Roz Eisenberg; Jody Ellis; Father Bernard Gerbus, O.F.M.; Richard Halford; E. B. and Jane Hall; Connie Hernández; Emily Hughes; John

Kessell; Father Otto Krische, O.F.M.; Kate McGraw; Doris Maiorano; Robert Martin; Jim Maryol; N. Scott Momaday; Phyllis Morgan; Marcia Muth; Ambassador Frank V. Ortiz, Jr.; Carlos Felix Pacheco; Donna Quasthoff; Pedro Ribera-Ortega; Father Guadalupe Rivera; Father Jack Clark Robinson, O.F.M.; Father Juan Romero; Father Gilbert Schneider, O.F.M.; Dr. Randolph Seligman; Julia Silva; Marc Simmons; Mónica Sosaya-Halford; Father Thomas Steele, S.J.; Stuart Udall; Anna Mae Vigil; Jim Walsh; R. C. "Doc" Weaver; and Malcolm Withers.

I am especially grateful to Fray Angélico's brothers and sisters who provided insights into his life and work over the course of several interviews: Nora Chávez, Fabián Chávez, Judge Antonio Chávez, José Chávez, Francisco Eugenio Chávez, and Adela Montoya. The generosity and friendship of Fred Grillo, one of Fray Angélico's dear friends, have given me a first-hand understanding of the loving support he and his wife Marguerite offered Fray Angélico for many years.

INTRODUCTION

A Rose for Fray Angélico Chávez: Homage to
New Mexico's Foremost Twentieth-Century Humanist

ELLEN McCRACKEN

In his beautiful and enduring story "A Rose for Emily," William Faulkner exquisitely crafted words, sentences, and images as the petals of a rose that would offer tribute to a lost stalwart of the Southern antebellum aristocracy. In their own version of this gesture, the writers and academics who have contributed to this volume of essays on the great New Mexico writer Fray Angélico Chávez offer petals in equal sincerity even if they are less artistic in vision and craft. How do admirers adequately acknowledge and pay tribute to the accomplishments of a renaissance man who, imbued with Franciscan humility, consistently eschewed praise and attention? To focus on some of his best-known works—*Clothed with the Sun* (1939), *New Mexico Triptych* (1940), *La Conquistadora: The Autobiography of an Ancient Statue* (1954), *Origins of New Mexico Families* (1954), *The Virgin of Port Lligat* (1959), or *My Penitente Land* (1974)— would present only a small part of his vast production over seven decades.[1] Instead, proceeding from several of the fields in which Fray Angélico Chávez worked—history, biography, literature, art, and religion—the ten essays written for this book sample a wide range of his contributions, making a small attempt at paying homage to his life and work of intellectual rigor, scholarly commitment, and artistic prowess.

Chávez's early formation bears the signs of the wide-ranging intellectual he would become. Manuel Ezequiel Chávez was born on April 10, 1910, in the small northern New Mexico town of Wagon Mound, the first of ten children of Fabián Chávez and María Nicolasa Roybal de Chávez. In 1912 his family moved to San Diego, California, where his father worked as a carpenter for the Panama-California Exposition; there Manuel came into contact with the important role of the Franciscans in the history of the Americas, exemplified in mission architecture and the legacy of figures such as Fray Junípero Serra. After his family's return to New Mexico, he was educated in the local public school in Mora by the Sisters of Loretto. He read prolifically, following the example of his parents, who recited poetry and left copies of the newspaper *El nuevo mexicano* for him to read; at a neighbor's house he spent hours reading *National Geographic* magazine supplemented by his family's encyclopedia, which he read from cover to cover, and the Spanish primers his parents had used. During his grammar school years, he did pencil and pen drawings and watercolor paintings. His family remembers that one day in fourth or fifth grade he announced to the class that he wanted to become the first Franciscan native to New Mexico. A few years later, during a mission given by the charismatic Franciscan friar Father Jerome Hesse in Mora, Chávez spoke to the visiting priest about his own desire to become a Franciscan, cultivated by his early experience in San Diego and his reading about the history of the Franciscans in New Mexico. At the age of fourteen, shortly after his family moved to Santa Fe, Chávez was accepted for seminary studies in Cincinnati.[2]

As a native Spanish speaker who had learned English in school, Chávez was self-conscious about his English when he entered the seminary and strove to compete with his fellow students in the use of their language by avidly studying the classic literary works in English.[3] He began to produce prose, drama, essays, verse, drawing, and painting in this period. In the *Brown and White,* the seminary magazine of which he would eventually become editor, he published his first poem at age fifteen and in February 1928 his first story, "A Desert Idyll," in which he paid tribute to his mentor, Fr. Jerome Hesse. A talented member of the first class to study and live in the new seminary building at Mount Healthy, Chávez was allowed to embellish the bare walls with paintings he made of Saint Francis and Saint Anthony. In view of this and his other artwork, upon entering the novitiate in 1929 he was named after the fifteenth-century painter Fra Angelico da Fiesole.

His creativity burgeoned on many fronts during the years of strict religious formation in preparation for the priesthood and was frequently overlain with the impish sense of humor that persisted throughout his life. When allowed to repaint the image of Saint Anthony in Saint Francis Seminary, for example, he painted the saint with the face of a beautiful Mexican movie star popular at the time. He published under playful pseudonyms such as "Ann Jellicoe"; wrote, directed, and acted in satiric plays; and wrote humorous verses and essays for the seminary magazine. And even while a seminarian he cultivated his strong interest in history, publishing essays in student publications and, from 1934–

40, a humorous monthly column on Franciscan history for the national Catholic magazine *St. Anthony Messenger.*

The rigors of seminary training were compounded for Chávez by his long distance from home and the large cultural gap between the predominantly German milieu of the Cincinnati seminary and his own Hispanic New Mexican background. Nonetheless, his intelligence, discipline, creativity, and deep religious commitment enabled him to excel during his thirteen years of preparation in Ohio, Michigan, and Indiana, and in 1937 he was ordained at Saint Francis Cathedral in Santa Fe, the first native-born New Mexican to become a Franciscan friar. In subsequent years his priestly ministry included assignments at Peña Blanca and its missions; Jémez; Cerrillos; as military chaplain during World War II in the Philippines and in Germany in the early 1950s; and later as archdiocesan archivist. From the time of his first assignment at Peña Blanca on, he continued the dedication and discipline of the seminary years, producing a vast quantity of artistic, literary, and scholarly work, sometimes sleeping only three or four hours a night. His wide-ranging cultural production includes restoration, painting, drawing, poetry, fiction, journalism, genealogy, biography, philology, translation, and revisionist historical texts based on copious archival research.

To note that Fray Angélico wrote twenty-three books and over six hundred other pieces in his career of over seven decades, most of which was also spent in active priestly ministry, merely scratches the surface of his extraordinary contributions to twentieth-century American letters. This volume begins to probe the richness that underlies the quantitative record of Chávez's achievement. In March 1996, four of the contributors (García, Steele, McCracken, and Chávez) presented papers on Fray Angélico's work at the meeting of the Pacific Coast and Rocky Mountain Councils of Latin American Studies in Santa Fe, which took place, in an unexpected convergence of circumstances, three days after Chávez's death. Subsequently, other writers and scholars agreed to write essays for this volume, enabling a multidisciplinary foray into some of the pivotal aspects of Chávez's life and work. While much remains to be written on Chávez's accomplishments, this book focuses on his achievements as an historian, a literary and artistic figure, and a Franciscan.

In the opening essay, Southwest historian Marc Simmons tells the story of Chávez's engagement with the researching and writing of history after his ordination in 1937. Although Chávez had published several historical pieces in Franciscan venues in the 1930s and 1940s, in 1948 he began to publish his research in scholarly journals and books. Simmons documents the path of development of Chávez's career as an historian, his initial work in the poorly organized archdiocesan records, his training under the eminent Spanish colonial historian France V. Scholes, and the early recognition accorded Chávez by experts in the field of Southwestern history. Near the end of his life, Chávez was recognized as one of the most distinguished scholars of colonial New Mexico history.

Mario T. García, an historian of American ethnic and race relations, approaches Chávez as an oppositional historian who counters the traditionally accepted master narrative of United States history in which northern European Protestant peoples are given center stage. Decades before the Chicano movement, García argues, Chávez's focus on religion and the role of Hispano Catholics was a means of recentering ethnic identity in the growing Anglo-American master historical narrative of the times. Chávez particularly emphasized non-official popular religious traditions and confraternities whose roots can be traced back to colonial Spanish times, and he reevaluated the roles of nineteenth-century clergy such as Archbishop Lamy, Father Machebeuf, Padre Martínez, and Padre Gallegos.

Literary historian Luis Leal focuses on Fray Angélico's work in the late 1940s on the history of La Conquistadora, the statue that, as Chávez documented, was brought to New Mexico in 1625 by Fray Alonso de Benavides. Leal returns to some of the same sources Chávez had used fifty years earlier and examines Chávez's innovative 1954 book *La Conquistadora: The Autobiography of an Ancient Statue* in the context of Spanish and Latin American literary traditions. Primarily a work of history, this hybrid text overlays the historical narrative with fictional trappings to bring history alive for readers. Chávez's original aim in historical research was to distinguish fact from fiction, but here he playfully merges fact with fiction in an ingenious personification of an inanimate object.

Father Thomas J. Steele, a cultural historian and critic, opens the section devoted to Chávez's literature and art with an analysis of the role of miraculous or marvelous events and personages in Fray Angélico's short stories. He situates the depiction of the extraordinary in Chávez's stories in the context of European philosophy and theology, American Romanticism, and the Hispano traditions of New Mexico. Presenting a taxonomy of Chávez's fictive depictions of the marvelous, Fr. Steele also uses his expertise on the tradition of New Mexican *santos* to analyze the religious visual images that structure Chávez's stories.

Examining the strong interrelation of the visual and the verbal throughout Fray Angélico's work, literary and cultural critic Ellen McCracken argues that Chávez's cultural production constitutes a harmonious continuum of various forms of visual/verbal hybridity, all of which are linked by a compelling impulse to narrate. At the strongly verbal end of the continuum, in poems, essays, and novels, Fray Angélico uses "visible language" to make readers see; in entirely visual works, such as the frescoes at Peña Blanca, implicit verbal narrative plays a strong role; and his many composite visual/verbal works, such as book seals and writings with his own illustrations, invite readers to enjoy a harmony essential to narrative development.

Literary critic Manuel Martín-Rodríguez focuses on Chávez's masterpiece, *The Virgin of Port Lligat,* which joins themes from art, theology, classical mythology, nuclear physics, and astronomy in a unifying allegorical network. As a Franciscan priest, Chávez turns the somewhat vague religious references in Dalí's surrealistic painting "The Madonna of Port Lligat" into a carefully constructed allegory of the divine. Nonetheless, Chávez's book opens up a number of alternative readings that undermine this unifying allegorical attempt, Martín-Rodríguez argues; the poetic closure the text seeks is ultimately subverted by its own intertextual openness.

Probing further the importance of Spain and Spanish culture in Chávez's work, literary scholar and translator Clark Colahan studies the classic book *My Penitente Land.* Both here and in his fiction and genealogy, Fray Angélico broadens the concept of aristocracy by arguing that, regardless of their social class, those in New Mexico who have inherited authentic Spanish culture are heirs to a noble legacy. Colahan argues that just as early-twentieth-century Mexican writers and artists embraced Aztec culture as a means of asserting cultural resistance to the Spanish conquest, so does a figure such as Chávez embrace Spanish culture as a reaction against the U.S. takeover of New Mexico. Central to Fray Angélico's attraction to Spain is its unique religious tradition and spirituality.

The final section of this volume focuses on the life of Fray Angélico Chávez and his relationship to Franciscanism. Father Jack Clark Robinson argues that to understand Chávez as a professional writer, historian, or artist, one must first understand his profession of the life of a Franciscan. In a compelling narrative based on an interview with Chávez and archival research in Cincinnati and New Mexico, Fr. Robinson narrates some of the key moments in Chávez's seminary years and his missionary work in New Mexico after ordination. Writing as a member of the order himself, Robinson moves beyond a chronological account to present rich details of the everyday life and milieu in which Chávez blossomed as a friar.

Father Murray Bodo, a Franciscan poet from Gallup now ministering, teaching, and writing in Cincinnati, brings his expertise on the life and thought of Saint Francis to his account of the role of the saint in Fray Angélico's work. Although Chávez wrote many tributes to Saint Francis, he particularly identified with the stigmatic Francis, perhaps because of the tension in his life between his Franciscan formation in Ohio, Michigan, and Indiana and his

Hispanic roots in New Mexico. The figure of the Bird of Perfect Joy, central to the story of the stigmata, liberates Franciscan spirituality from the popular, sentimental image of Francis speaking to the birds, instead emphasizing the image of the six-winged Seraph above Christ. Aficionados of Fray Angélico's work will remember his stunning mural depicting this image (see Fig. 5.4).

In the final essay, Thomas E. Chávez, colonial historian and Fray Angélico's nephew, recounts some of his memories of Chávez, developed through personal and professional contact with his uncle over several decades. Details emerge about the older Chávez's unofficial mentorship of his nephew's development as a historian, anecdotes about everyday life, and several of the paintings Fray Angélico did throughout the years, in particular the story of the destruction of the frescoes at Peña Blanca.

These essays begin to probe the expansive contributions of Chávez's life and work. They depart from and go beyond the unequivocal statements of authorities in the fields in which Chávez worked, such as Father Thomas Steele, "Chávez's pronouncements about the religious history and culture of Hispanic New Mexico are probably going to endure like the dialogues of Plato, to which all later western philosophy has been mere footnote"; New Mexico state historian Myra Ellen Jenkins: "When it comes to [C]hurch matters in the colonial period and to genealogy, he is the source. He is the definitive authority"; historian Marc Simmons: "He is New Mexico's foremost man of letters in the 20th century."[4] And indeed, Fray Angélico's life work broadens the usual notion of the humanist by adding the dimension of his commitment to serving humanity in the many years of his ministry as a Franciscan missionary.

The story of this stellar figure of New Mexican letters and his effect on American thought and culture is itself an expanding narrative that will be carried forward by many sectors of the public in years to come. Scholars, writers, and researchers will continue to find in his work a myriad of intriguing paths to pursue and enlarge upon; the visual material culture with which he beautified and enriched northern New Mexico will carry his legacy to future generations, as will his popular genealogies and historical works; and the widespread interest in multiculturalism and historical recovery across the U.S. will lead many to come to know his work and its important contribution to American letters.

NOTES

1. Even the title of a volume such as this compresses his life and work into three summary words which only inadequately convey his contributions. To omit his key role as a historian is perhaps unpardonable, but the full list of the areas in which he worked would defy the limits of a functional title.

2. Kate McGraw, "About to Turn 80, Poet-Priest Still Busy," *Santa Fe New Mexican,* 8 April 1990, p. A-1+; "Vignette: Fray Angélico Chávez," *The Santa Fean* (Apr.–May 1975), pp. 6–7; Nasario García, "In Passing: Fray Angélico Chávez (Manuel Ezequiel Chávez), 1910–1996," *New Mexico Historical Review* (July 1996), pp. 269–73; William E. Barrett, "Poet in a Ghost Town," *Catholic Digest,* 24 (Oct. 1960), pp. 93–98; author's interviews with Fabián Chávez, 9 Aug. 1996, and Nora Chávez, 13 Aug. 1996.

3. See Barrett, op. cit., and the essay Chávez published as a fifteen-year-old seminarian, "Seeing the World Through Authors' Eyes," *Brown and White* 2 (March 1926), pp. 1–3, in which he analyzes in detail the pleasures of the books read in his first-semester English class.

4. Thomas J. Steele, "Foreword," Fray Angélico Chávez, *My Penitente Land: Reflections on Spanish New Mexico* (Santa Fe: Museum of New Mexico Press, 1993), p. vii; Myra Ellen Jenkins and Marc Simmons, quoted in Malinda Elliott, "Fray Angélico Chávez: Telling the History of New Mexico in a Personal Way," *Santa Fe Reporter, Good News,* Feb. 28, 1980, p. 15.

PART 1

HISTORICAL RECOVERY

CHAPTER ONE

FRAY ANGÉLICO CHÁVEZ: THE MAKING OF A MAVERICK HISTORIAN

MARC SIMMONS
Cerrillos, New Mexico

Of his many contributions to diverse fields of human endeavor, Fray Angélico Chávez probably will be remembered longest for his achievements in the writing of regional history. Like his other creative pursuits, this one bore the stamp of his highly individualistic personality—an anomaly in itself, since he came from the conservative and traditional Hispanic culture of northern New Mexico and spent much of his life as a Franciscan friar, bound by the rules of the order.

From his initial experience as a historian Fray Angélico developed a personal sense of mission: he believed that the largely unknown Hispanic settlers of the upper Rio Grande Valley had engaged for centuries in an extraordinary enterprise and that the record of their activity was worth recovery and dissemination. In short, he aimed at telling the story of the early-day New Mexicans from his perspective as an insider.

In assessing Fray Angélico's career as a historian, it is worth examining the circumstances that led to his intense interest in his homeland's past. From that, a review can be made of some of his more important works and of the standing accorded to him by professional historians.

Growing up in the communities of Wagon Mound and Mora, New Mexico, where his first language was Spanish, Fray Angélico developed what would prove a lifelong devotion to his Hispanic heritage. Attracted by the intellectual and spiritual sides of life, he gravitated toward the Franciscan order, the one that had ministered to the people of New Mexico since 1598. Following a novitiate, he made his solemn vows in that religious body in 1933 and four years later was ordained a priest at Santa Fe's Saint Francis Cathedral.[1]

Shortly afterward he was assigned to the parish of Peña Blanca, south of Santa Fe, which included the Indian missions at Cochiti, Santo Domingo, and San Felipe. There he was pleased to minister to the rural folk, with whom he always felt a close affinity. But the isolated station also gave him the opportunity to pursue personal projects and interests, including creative writing and publishing poems and short stories, mostly of a religious nature, that were praised by critics.

During World War II, Fray Angélico volunteered for the U.S. Army Chaplains' Corps and underwent basic training at the Chaplain School in Harvard University. He was sent to the Pacific theater and participated in the bloody assault landings on Guam and at Leyte, in the Philippines. Long afterward he would quip, "I wanted a Purple Heart, but I was too skinny for the Japanese to hit."[2] Upon being demobilized in 1946 with the rank of major, he returned to Santa Fe and took up new duties at the cathedral.

During his years of service he had continued to write poems and, perhaps longing for his beloved New Mexico, had begun to think more seriously about its history. Once home, he conceived the idea of authoring a history of New Mexico's Franciscan missions.[3] In the mid-1930s, Archbishop Rudolph A. Gerken had called in the scattered records of the Catholic Church that still remained in the individual parishes and had founded an archdiocesan archives at the cathedral. Upon examining this material in 1947, Fray Angélico found it in great disorder, and he started loosely organizing the documents in topical bundles. He made slow progress owing to his lack of training in reading Spanish paleography and in formal archival methods.[4]

Before long, however, he was bitten by the documentary bug. As he delved deeper into the old brittle papers with their fading ink, he became fascinated with two new subjects: the genealogy and history of his own Chávez family and the other early families who had put down permanent roots along the Rio Grande, and the origins and history of the Marian image brought to New Mexico in colonial times and known as La Conquistadora. These interests soon absorbed him, and his original resolve to produce a general history of the local Franciscan missions faded, never to be revived. Chávez himself gave the reason for that abandonment: After several years of archival digging, he had discovered only scant information on the missionaries, while his notes on the lay pioneers drawn from baptismal, marriage, and death certificates, together with ancillary documents, had piled up considerably. In his words, "It was like the case of a miner who sifted a hill of ore for gold, setting aside any silver he encountered; in the end the silver far outweighed the gold. The only thing to do was to render the silver useful."[5]

Already endowed with an abiding affection and respect for the native folk of his New Mexico, Fray Angélico now saw that he had an opportunity to illuminate their past in all its rich and dramatic dimensions. Like his missionary work as a Franciscan, his scholarly labors would be another form of public service, opening long-sealed chambers of history and revealing to New Mexicans knowledge of their forbears that they had assumed was lost. As a bonus, Fray Angélico had discovered that historical investigation was intellectually challenging, and also just plain fun. This pursuit would occupy him almost to the end of his life.

The culmination of his genealogical studies, begun in 1947, was the book *Origins of New Mexico Families,* published by the Historical Society of New Mexico in 1954. Fray Angélico described it as a "comprehensive, if incomplete, record of the original Spanish families."[6] The volume was instantly recognized as an indispensable research tool, and copies were eagerly snatched up by New Mexicans newly fired with zeal to trace their roots. Weighing the merits of *Origins* in a review, New Mexican author Erna Fergusson commented that it "explodes a few myths and is replete with hints . . . of what life was really like in Spain's New Mexico."[7] Her observation points up one of the hallmarks of Fray Angélico's historical work—his unflagging honesty. Even when questioning some of his more daring interpretations, readers can see that he strictly adhered to the rules of evidence and never shirked from drawing conclusions that might prove unpopular.

At the beginning of his historical career, Fray Angélico had published a brief article on Don Fernando Durán de Chávez, one of the earliest members of his family to settle in New Mexico.[8] In *Origins* he presented a more extended treatment of the Chávezes during the seventeenth and eighteenth centuries. And finally in 1989 he returned to the subject again in one of his last books, titled *Chávez, A Distinctive American Clan of New Mexico.*[9] His aim was to highlight the significant role played by his ancestors in the planting and flowering of Hispanic civilization in this corner of the empire.

Concurrent with beginning his genealogical studies in 1947, Fray Angélico commenced a search for documentary evidence that might establish the true history of the statue of the Virgin Mary called La Conquistadora. This small figure of willow wood had become an object of special devotion among New Mexicans, who, while acknowledging her antiquity, possessed no information about her origins. As to its significance, Archbishop Edwin Vincent Byrne referred to La Conquistadora as "the very soul of the Spanish Southwest."[10]

Popular tradition credited General Diego de Vargas with first bringing the statue to Santa Fe at the time of the Reconquest of upper New Mexico from the rebellious Pueblo Indians, 1692–93. By the 1940s, however, no documents had yet surfaced that could lend credence to that story. Indeed, several prominent scholars expressed the opinion that La Conquistadora was probably a fairly modern creation and certainly did not date back to the late seventeenth century. Roswell, New Mexico author Cleve Hallenbeck in his book *Legends of the Spanish Southwest* included a sympathetic chapter on the subject but judged La Conquistadora's story as largely made up of legend.[11]

The doubt cast upon the authenticity of the statue pained Fray Angélico Chávez greatly. It implied that his fellow New Mexicans could not keep their history straight, and, even more damaging, that their religion was tainted by a fable. As he continued to rummage through masses of colonial documentation, he kept a vigilant eye in hopes of encountering some clue to resolve the mystery.

One Sunday in May 1947, Fray Angélico appeared for morning Mass in the sacristy of the cathedral. On such occasions he was usually very solemn, preparing himself spiritually for the service. But on this day, the acolytes noticed that he was smiling and quite happy. He even volunteered an explanation: "I've found that La Conquistadora was *not* a pious legend after all. My Mass today will be a thanksgiving for that discovery!"[12]

About this time Fray Angélico came across some fragmentary documents in the archdiocesan archives that referred to the existence of the confraternity of La Conquistadora (then called Nuestra Señora del Rosario) and to the body's *mayordomo,* or president, Francisco Gómez Robledo. The New Mexicans at the time these documents were written, 1684, were living in exile in the El Paso Valley, following the disaster of the Pueblo Revolt of 1680. This revelation pushed the presence of La Conquistadora back well before the Vargas Reconquest period. Very quickly other documentary discoveries followed.[13] Nevertheless, the El Paso records do not seem to have been the ones that led Fray Angélico to celebrate his Mass of thanksgiving.

Scholars had been aware since 1916, when his *Memorial* on New Mexican affairs was first translated and published in English, that Father Alonso de Benavides had brought a statue of the Virgin to New Mexico when he came in 1625 to assume charge of the Franciscan missions.[14] Fray Angélico had begun to suspect that this was the image that in time was given the title La Conquistadora and that now rested in her own side chapel at the cathedral. But was there any way to verify this theory?

Then, in the spring of 1947, he obtained a copy of a document from the Archive of the Indies in Seville, Spain, concerning Benavides's 1625 trip from Mexico City to Santa Fe. Among the freight consigned to the wagon train was a crate "in which the Virgin went, a *vara* and a quarter long and three-quarters wide and two thirds high." No mention of any other statue of the Virgin for this period had ever been found, leading Fray Angélico to propose that this particular image was, indeed, most likely La Conquistadora. The idea eventually won general acceptance.[15]

Pedro Ribera-Ortega, one of the cathedral acolytes in 1947, stated in a 1996 interview that it was the document giving the dimensions of the Virgin's traveling crate that had prompted Fray Angélico's elation and his celebration of the thanksgiving Mass. After measuring the actual image in the cathedral, he concluded, "The Conquistadora statue would fit quite snugly into such a box, with enough inches to spare all around for protective packing." While admitting that this was not conclusive proof, he believed that he had solved the question of the famous image's arrival date in New Mexico.[16]

A year later Fray Angélico published a detailed two-part article in the *New Mexico Historical Review,* under the title "Nuestra Señora del Rosario La Conquistadora," presenting his voluminous archival findings on the subject.[17] Immediately afterward, the Historical Society of New Mexico brought out the articles as a separate book, *Our Lady of the Conquest,* embellished with additional illustrations. Upon this, the legitimacy of La Conquistadora as a religious icon and a historical artifact was firmly established. As a result, her long-lapsed confraternity was revived, and she was blessed in 1960 with a papal coronation.

For Fray Angélico, his studies transcended mere academic history; they also had implications for religion and for the cultural survival of his people. The spirit of La Conquistadora he described as "Spanish in concept and feeling . . . Catholic to the core, being founded on, and quickened by, an especially Spanish-Catholic filial devotion towards the Mother of God."[18] Here can be seen an expression of his sense of *Hispanidad* (Spanishness), so strong among New Mexicans of his generation. That sentiment would guide the course of all his later historical writings and receive definitive treatment in his lyrical, interpretive book, *My Penitente Land, Reflections on Spanish New Mexico.*[19]

In late 1946 or early 1947, Fray Angélico struck up an acquaintance with Dr. France V. Scholes, professor of history and dean of the graduate school at the University of New Mexico, Albuquerque. A graduate of Harvard and a former head of the Division of Historical Research, Carnegie Institution of Washington, Scholes had come to the Southwest for his health in 1924. He was a Spanish colonialist, already recognized as an authority on Hispanic paleography.[20] The friendship that developed between the two men, based on their common research interests, would prove crucial to the education and advancement of Fray Angélico in the field of history.

In a revealing letter to Scholes, dated January 20, 1948, Fray Angélico wrote, in part:

Am anxious to see the Duran y Chavez references you are preparing for me, and most grateful for the trouble you are going into. I went with a fine comb through the fat Tierras vol. you had sent up to the Museum Library and am almost finished with my second trip through the Processo contra Gomez which I brought along. If the opportunity presents itself (free time and a car), you might see me soon. Again, mil gracias![21]

It is clear that Scholes was assisting Fray Angélico in the pursuit of his two current research projects: Chávez genealogy and the history of La Conquistadora. The court case against Gómez, for instance, was of interest because it dealt with Francisco Gómez Robledo, the *mayordomo* of the Cofradía de La Conquistadora in 1684. For years, Scholes had been reading documents and taking detailed notes on file cards. Whenever he received a new query from Fray Angélico, he consulted that resource, typed up a summary, and mailed it to Santa Fe.[22] He also sent him noncirculating material from the university library's special collections, something he managed to do by pulling rank. For a number of years, New Mexico historians had been visiting the main archives of Spain and Mexico in search of documentation relevant to their area. Every time they uncovered a *legajo* (bundle) of New Mexico items, they had it photocopied and the copies shipped back to the library in Albuquerque, where they were placed in heavy volumes bound in red buckram.

The fat *Tierras* volume, mentioned by Chávez in his letter of January 20, was one of those. *Tierras* was the name of a *ramo*, or branch, of the Archivo General de la Nación in Mexico City. Its focus was on early settlement and land tenure matters. As a courtesy, Scholes had arranged to have that book, and no doubt others like it, sent to the History Library of the Palace of the Governors, located on the Santa Fe plaza and thus very accessible to Fray Angélico. Scholes's willingness to accommodate can be taken as a measure of his esteem for the budding Franciscan scholar.

In 1947 Fray Angélico had published two thin historical pieces in *El Palacio,* the journal of the Museum of New Mexico. While he would later characterize them "as being quite faulty," they represented his entry into the formal discipline of history.[23] For his next article, "The Gallegos Relación Reconsidered," appearing in the *New Mexico Historical Review* (January 1948), he had to make no apologies and in fact received well-merited praise from some prominent professors.

Hernán Gallegos was a member and official chronicler of a small expedition composed of three Franciscans and a handful of soldiers that explored New Mexico in 1581–82. A translation of his *Relación,* or official journal, had come out in the *New Mexico Historical Review* in 1927, edited by the distinguished academics George P. Hammond and Agapito Rey. Another leading scholar, J. Lloyd Mecham, also published some collateral documents that cast light on the expedition.[24] With his newly acquired expertise, Fray Angélico read, or perhaps reread, the Gallegos *Relación* and found it wanting. His critical insight was born, as he put it, because of "one of those sudden hunches, unscientific perhaps in historical research, yet most helpful and psychologically lawful."[25] The more he studied the text, the firmer became his conviction that Gallegos was of "hypocritical and obsequious character" and that in several important instances he was "lying for his own ends."[26]

Fray Angélico mildly, even apologetically, took his predecessors to task for taking at face value some of Hernán Gallegos's bald assertions. "This paper," he declared in his conclusion, "was not meant to criticize my betters, whose historical spade-work I not only admire but depend on; rather, I want to show how the author of the contemporary documents in question cannot be trusted implicitly in all he writes."[27] This, in effect, was a declaration of his future modus operandi: he would mine original documents and formulate his own conclusions and interpretations.

Scholes read "The Gallegos Relación Reconsidered" and was impressed. The next time he saw Fray Angélico he told him that he had a bright future as a historian of colonial New Mexico. Chávez replied that his only formal training was in European and Church history. Scholes offered to teach him the mechanics of paleography and the fine points of archival investigation. Fray Angélico now had an automobile, and for the next several years he drove one or two afternoons a week down to Albuquerque to receive private tutoring in Scholes's living room. More than thirty years later he would remark, "I got all that wonderful education from Scholes for free."[28]

Another person who read his Gallegos article with interest was the dean of Spanish borderlands scholars, Herbert Eugene Bolton of the University of California, Berkeley, who was also the biographer of Coronado. Fray Angélico had gone to the Bancroft Library there in 1950 to engage in research, aided, as he put it, by "a minor scholarship" from the Historical Society of New Mexico. He met Bolton, who immediately recalled reading "The Gallegos Relación Reconsidered." "That's right, Fray Angélico," he said. "Give 'em hell!"[29] Both Hammond and Mecham, who had been gently reproached therein, were former graduate students of Bolton. The incident suggests that Chávez by this early date had won admission to the select fraternity of Southwest historians.

During his years with Scholes, Fray Angélico was allowed to use freely his mentor's hefty card files, from which he extracted innumerable biographical references that ended up as citations in *Origins of New Mexico Families*. In 1989, he wondered aloud where those valuable files had gone upon the death of Scholes in 1979.[30]

Another remarkable opportunity fell into Fray Angélico's lap during his tutoring days. It had its origins in the winter of 1927–28, when a young France Scholes was researching in Mexico City's archives. During a chance meeting with Mrs. Adolph Bandelier, she informed him of some unknown New Mexico documents rumored to be in storage at Mexico's Biblioteca Nacional (National Library). Upon checking, Scholes discovered ten *legajos* of New Mexican items, which he arranged to have photographed by the Library of Congress in 1930. From those photographs, an additional set of copies was made for the University of New Mexico Library.[31]

Included in the collection was a thick manuscript written by Fray Francisco Atanasio Domínguez that described his ecclesiastical inspection of all New Mexico's missions and churches in the years 1776 to 1777. In addition to his formal comments, it included candid observations on domestic life and customs in the province, making it an extremely useful source. Earlier historians had completely overlooked the document.

About 1943, while Fray Angélico was away at war as an army chaplain, Dr. Scholes called the Domínguez report to the attention of his research associate, Eleanor B. Adams, who was also a member of the history faculty at the University of New Mexico. She took on the task of transcribing the document with the intention of translating and annotating it for publication. But Adams was a slow and quiet worker, and nothing more was heard from her on the matter for the next several years.[32]

By the time Scholes was receiving Fray Angélico in his living room in the early fifties, he had completely forgotten what Miss Adams was doing, or even that he had introduced her to Domínguez. Therefore, one afternoon he handed another copy of the manuscript to Fray Angélico and persuaded him to undertake a translation. Chávez threw himself into the project with enthusiasm.

Months later, Adams discovered what had happened and was furious, not at Chávez, but at Scholes for his impaired memory. Fray Angélico contacted her and gallantly offered to turn over to her what he had done so far and withdraw. Although of a prickly nature, Adams was also fair minded, and she was unwilling to see the problem settled in that way. After some discussion, they agreed to cooperate and produce a book jointly.

The result was a volume far superior to what either one could have done independently, since each brought unique qualifications and different background material to the effort. Released in 1956 by the University of New Mexico Press, the *Missions of New Mexico, 1776* was a handsome oversized book

Figure 1.1 Eleanor B. Adams, France V. Scholes, and Fray Angélico Chávez at the University of New Mexico Press in 1956 at the time of publication of Missions of New Mexico, 1776 *(courtesy of John Kessell)*

that promptly won acknowledgment as a standard source on the eighteenth century. Much to the pleasure of the patriotic Fray Angélico, it was reissued in 1976 as part of New Mexico's contribution to the American bicentennial.[33]

As the book was going to press in 1956, one other point of contention arose. Adams telephoned Fray Angélico and demanded to know whose name was going to appear first on the dust jacket and title page, hers or his. Graciously, he replied, "Why, alphabetically Adams comes before Chávez. And besides, I was always taught, ladies first!" Adams was mollified and ever after spoke of Fray Angélico in glowing terms. Her anger toward Scholes had also cooled; she gave permission for the dedication page to read "To France Vinton Scholes, His Book." For Chávez, that dedication probably represented a partial repayment for all the instruction he had received, and for which he always remained grateful.

By then Fray Angélico was securely established as a major regional historian. He continued to pour forth a stream of popular and scholarly articles and, of course, more books. Three of his new works were published by the Academy of American Franciscan History in Washington, D.C.: a documentary catalog, *Archives of the Archdiocese of Santa Fe, 1678–1900* (1957); a new look at the Franciscans accompanying the Coronado expedition, *Coronado's Friars* (1968); and a work on sixteenth-century Mexican history, *The Oroz Codex* (1972). Also, as a further contribution to the bicentennial he prepared a new translation of *The Domínguez-Escalante Journal*, describing a major expedition west of New Mexico in 1776. It was published by Brigham Young University Press in 1976.

Toward the end of his life, Fray Angélico found difficulty in placing his specialized history titles with publishers. Times were changing, reading as a pastime was in decline, and few persons seemed interested any longer in the minutiae associated with the story of Hispanic New Mexico. His last three books were self-published, the funds raised by him from private sponsors or drawn from his own meager savings. On his eightieth birthday, in 1990, he told a journalist that he had lost several thousand dollars on these ventures, and consequently he had decided to stop writing.[35]

By the sheer force of his drive and personality, Fray Angélico forged a career as a historian, and he had done so in the face of daunting obstacles and hardships. Pardonably, he appeared to enjoy his modest fame because it suggested that he had met with some success in raising public awareness of his state's Hispanic heritage. The Reverend Donald Starkey, chancellor of the Archdiocese, said of him, "Except for Father Chávez, I can't think of a Southwestern priest since Father Junípero Serra [of California] who has shouldered the heavy burden of ministry to the people while at the same time exercising great creative talents."[36]

As a self-motivated, independent thinker, Fray Angélico delighted in identifying historical puzzles that academic scholars had ignored or avoided. He would burrow into piles of archival material, discover pieces long buried, reconstruct or revise our pictures of the past, and then, when his publications produced controversy, as they often did, he would smile sweetly and grant another interview to the press.

A prime example was the lead article he wrote for the *New Mexico Historical Review* (April, 1967). Titled "Pohé-yemo's Representative and the Pueblo Revolt of 1680," it advanced the startling proposition that the bloody uprising had been designed and led not by a San Juan Indian called Popé, as long supposed, but by a secret figure named Naranjo. According to Fray Angélico, he was "a big Negro or black-complexioned mulatto . . . who insinuated himself among the ritual leaders of the Pueblos" and claimed to be a lieutenant of one of the native deities, Pohé-yemo, the Sun Bringer.[37] The article occasioned a storm, particularly among the Pueblo Indians, some of whom charged Fray Angélico with racism. His words, they felt, made it appear that the Pueblos were not smart enough to plan and execute their own revolt without the assistance of someone from the Old World. Commenting on the furor much later, Fray Angélico said, "I was called a 'false historian' and much worse. I think the [modern-day] Indians wanted to keep the credit for their own leaders."[38] In reality, Fray Angélico had built his thesis on extremely tenuous evidence drawn by reading between the lines of seventeenth- and eighteenth-century documents. When fellow historians would refer to it as a theory, he bristled and insisted emphatically that he had proven his case.

This tendency toward inflexibility apparently failed to harm his standing among his colleagues. It did not quite amount to arrogance (his ingrained Franciscan humility prevented that), but rather it seemed to be a matter of his towering self-confidence crossing the line to become overconfidence.

Universities in his home state conferred honorary degrees upon Fray Angélico, the Historical Society of New Mexico presented him a lifetime achievement award in 1987, and state historian Myra Ellen Jenkins has termed him "our most distinguished scholar in the field of colonial New Mexico history."[39]

We are unlikely ever again to see anyone cast in his mold.

NOTES

1. "Fray Angélico Chávez," *El Palacio* 56 (Nov. 1949), p. 336.

2. Quoted in Richard B. Johnson, "A Genius of Sorts," *Empire Magazine* (of the *Denver Post*), Jan. 11, 1981, p. 20.

3. "Fray Angélico Chávez," p. 337. Before the war, Fray Angélico had published at least two historical pieces: a sketch of Coronado's friar, Fray Juan de Padilla, in "The Gold Hunters," *Franciscan Herald* 26 (Mar. 1938), pp. 269, 288; and a two-part history of New Mexico's Santo Domingo Indian pueblo titled "Santo Domingo," *The Provincial Chronicle* 14 (Fall 1941), pp. 5–14, and (Winter 1941–42), pp. 91–98. I thank Ellen McCracken for finding and sharing these references.

4. Fray Angélico Chávez, *Archives of the Archdiocese of Santa Fe, 1678–1900* (Washington, D.C.: Academy of American Franciscan History, 1957), p. 3.

5. Fray Angélico Chávez, *Origins of New Mexico Families* (Santa Fe: Historical Society of New Mexico, 1954), p. ix. In 1982, Fray Angélico deposited a manuscript in eleven notebooks entitled "New Mexico Roots Ltd." in the special collections of the University of New Mexico Library, Albuquerque. This work contains much genealogical information not found in *Origins of New Mexico Families*. Fray Angélico did publish a brief article, "A Resumé of Ecclesiastical History in New Mexico," *The Provincial Chronicle* 20 (Spring 1948), pp. 137–43. Reference courtesy of Ellen McCracken.

6. Ibid., p. x. Reprint editions were issued by the University of Albuquerque (Albuquer-

que: Calvin Horn, 1973) and by William Gannon (Santa Fe, 1975). A revised edition containing a new foreword by Thomas E. Chávez and an addendum, "New Names in New Mexico, 1820–1850," was released by the Museum of New Mexico Press, 1992.

7. *New Mexico Historical Review* 30 (July 1955), p. 255.

8. *El Palacio* 55 (April 1948), pp. 103–21.

9. Chávez, *A Distinctive American Clan of New Mexico* (Santa Fe: William Gannon, 1989).

10. Quoted in Pedro Ribera-Ortega, La Conquistadora: *America's Oldest Madonna* (Santa Fe: Sunstone Press, 1975), p. 4.

11. Cleve Hallenbeck, *Legends of the Spanish Southwest* (Glendale, Calif.: Arthur H. Clark, 1930), pp. 97–100. See also Fray Angélico Chávez, *Our Lady of the Conquest* (Santa Fe: Historical Society of New Mexico, 1948), pp. 2–3.

12. This account was obtained in two telephone interviews with Pedro Ribera-Ortega, one of the acolytes, July 6 and August 12, 1996. At this writing he remains *mayordomo* of the Confraternity of La Conquistadora.

13. Chávez, *Our Lady of the Conquest,* p. 5.

14. Ibid., 34.

15. The document was from the Contaduría section of the Archive of the Indies, *legajo* 726, according to Fray Angélico; see *Our Lady of the Conquest,* p. 34, n. 47.

16. Telephone interview, August 12, 1996; and, Chávez, *Our Lady of the Conquest,* p. 35.

17. Vol. 5 (April, 1948), pp. 94–128; and (July 1948), pp. 176–216.

18. Quoted in Ribera-Ortega, *La Conquistadora,* p. 5.

19. *My Penitente Land, Reflections on Spanish New Mexico* (Albuquerque: University of New Mexico Press, 1974).

20. For Scholes's background see Richard E. Greenleaf, "France Vinton Scholes, Historian of New Spain," *The Americas* 27 (Jan.1971), pp. 223–27.

21. A copy of this letter is in the Fray Angélico Chávez File, author's collection.

22. Chávez to Scholes, Santa Fe, Jan. 23, 1948, copy in Chávez File.

23. The quotation and the two articles are cited in Phyllis S. Morales, *Fray Angélico Chávez: A Bibliography of His Published Writings, 1925–1978* (Santa Fe: The Lightning Tree, 1980), p. 36.

24. J. Lloyd Mecham, "Supplementary Documents Relating to the Chamuscado-Rodríguez Expedition," *Southwestern Historical Quarterly* 29 (1925), pp. 224–31. The Hammond and Rey two-part translation of the *Relación* was printed in the *New Mexico Historical Review* 2 (July and Oct.1927), pp. 239–68; and 334–62.

25. Chávez, "The Gallegos Relación Reconsidered," p. 3.

26. Ibid., pp. 3, 6.

27. Ibid., p. 20.

28. Marc Simmons, interview with Fray Angélico Chávez, Santa Fe, Dec. 5, 1989.

29. Ibid. See also Fray Angélico Chávez, "Some Original New Mexico Documents in California Libraries," *New Mexico Historical Review* 25 (July 1950), p. 244.

30. Marc Simmons, interview with Fray Angélico Chávez, Santa Fe, Dec. 5, 1989. The Scholes papers and documents relating to Mexico went to Tulane University, New Orleans.

Those on New Mexico were deposited in the University of New Mexico Library, Albuquerque. The card files seem to have been lost.

31. Roland F. Dickey, "Paging Procrustes, An Adventure in the Making of a Book," *New Mexico Quarterly* 26 (Summer 1956), pp. 59–61; and France V. Scholes, "Manuscripts for the History of New Mexico in the National Library of Mexico City," *New Mexico Historical Review* 3 (July 1928), pp. 301–2.

32. Dickey, "Paging Procrustes," p. 62.

33. In addition to the second trade edition of 1976, a limited collectors' edition of 150 signed copies, hardbound and slipcased, were also issued.

34. Marc Simmons, interview with Fray Angélico Chávez, Santa Fe, Dec. 5, 1989.

35. *Santa Fe New Mexican,* April 8, 1990.

36. Johnson, "A Genius of Sorts," p. 19.

37. "Pohé-yemo's Representative and the Pueblo Revolt of 1680," pp. 89, 93.

38. William Hart, "Friar Dares to Debunk History," *Dallas Morning News,* Feb. 16, 1986, p. 47.

39. Ibid. and *La Crónica* [Newsletter of the Historical Society of New Mexico], no. 26 (Oct. 1987), pp. 1–2.

CHAPTER TWO

FRAY ANGÉLICO CHÁVEZ, RELIGIOSITY, AND NEW MEXICAN OPPOSITIONAL HISTORICAL NARRATIVE

MARIO T. GARCÍA
University of California, Santa Barbara

I

Since the 1960s the master historical narrative of the United States has been significantly challenged. This history proposes an America largely based on what can be termed the Anglo-American, Eastern-based ethnic experience. From this perspective, predominantly Protestant peoples of northern European descent are given center stage, especially in the formative years of the colonial era and early years of the republic.

Over the last three decades, however, oppositional narratives have surfaced that counter this predominant text with the intent of permitting other historical experiences and voices access into a reconstructed U.S. historical identity stressing not one major ethnic community but multiple ones. These revisions depicting the roles of Native Americans, African Americans, Spanish/ Mexican Americans, as well as Euro-American women and Euro-American working-class peoples are redefining American history. While not eliminating the Anglo-American story, they put it into perspective by recognizing the heterogeneous nature of the American saga.

In the Southwest, the challenge to this hegemonic narrative—as well as to its regional counterpart, which similarly extols the contributions of Anglo-Americans at the expense of other ethnic groups in the region—has come significantly from the development of Chicano historiography. Since the 1960s with the emergence of the militant and nationalist Chicano movement, historians, most of Chicano descent and identifying with the new stress on ethnic revitalization, have rewritten Southwestern history by calling attention to the major roles played by Mexican Americans in this area. Chicano historians are studying such themes as pre-U.S. communities and cultures, U.S. expansion and conquest, internal colonialism, Mexican immigration, the establishment of a Southwestern race, class, and gender system, the role of Mexican Americans in civil rights activities, and the importance of multiculturalism in the Southwest.

The new Chicano history also provides a new way of thinking about who makes history. It challenges the general notion of historical agency: the idea that primarily Anglo-Americans have made Southwestern history. By seeing Chicanos as people making history and struggling to control their own destinies, this historiography also counters the stereotype of Chicanos as being simply victims of history or, even worse, invisible in history. In fact, through their families, communities, churches, popular religious practices, and organized leadership, Chicanos have influenced the contours of Southwestern history and of American history.

While much of this oppositional historical revision has come in the wake of the Chicano movement of the late 1960s and early 1970s, there are important precursors. Chicano historiography has a genealogy that, while not as evident during the intense, politicized years as now, in what I call the post-Chicano movement period, is becoming more appreciated. Moving beyond the early militant ethnic nationalism, which stressed the radical roots of Chicano history, more recent writing recognizes the diversity of the Mexican-American experience in contrast to the previous concept of the "unified subject." This emphasis on difference has led to greater sensitivity and an acknowledgment of pre-movement writers and intellectuals who, in the context of their own historical periods, produced what can be interpreted as critical narratives as a way of countering Southwestern history that excluded, marginalized, or exoticized Spanish/Mexican contributions.

II

It is with this background in mind that I wish to interpret the historical writings of Fray Angélico Chávez, one of the most significant but in some ways least acknowledged historical critics in this country. This lack of recognition unfortunately extends to the area of Chicano studies, even though much of his work complements this field. In a writing career spanning seven decades, Chávez, a true renaissance man, produced some twenty-three published books including history, fiction, poetry as well as numerous articles, essays, and reviews. In addition, as a self-taught artist, Chávez created a range of religious and artistic images.

Concentrating on Fray Angélico's historical work, especially on the role of Hispano Catholics, I will suggest that Chávez's focus on religion was a way of asserting ethnic identity and opposing a growing Anglo-American historical presence that was pushing Chávez's subjects to the margins.

To understand Fray Angélico's stress on history and religion is to understand the historian himself. His writing of history contains a hidden and at times not so hidden autobiographical self. Born Manuel Ezequiel Chávez in Wagon Mound, New Mexico, on April 10, 1910, he descended from a long family line in New Mexico. Within his Hispano family traditions, Chávez was particularly shaped by his strong Catholic socialization that originated within his family. Beginning with his elementary schooling in Mora under the Sisters of Loretto, Chávez's entire education was largely at the hands of the Church. At age fourteen he chose a religious vocation and in 1924 commenced a long educational and training period in the Midwest to become an ordained member of the Franciscan order in 1937.

Because he displayed some talent in painting, he was given the religious name of Fray Angélico, after Fra Angelico, a medieval Dominican painter. Joining the Franciscans was a way of identifying with New Mexico's Spanish past, given the important role of the Franciscans in that history. "Everything I read about New Mexico," he would later tell an interviewer, "emphasized the Franciscans and their contributions to the country. I became attracted to them even though I had never seen one."[1]

Beginning in the 1940s, Fray Angélico began to systematically research the roots of the Hispano presence in New Mexico. Although not an academically trained historian, Chávez brought a rigorous and meticulous quality to his investigations. Not as readable as his other writings, his historical narratives, with the possible exception of *My Penitente Land,* are somewhat ponderous. Yet what these narratives lack in style, they more than make up in precise details.

Accepting the responsibility for historical accuracy, Chávez sought to understand and to educate himself as well as others about the non-Anglo, Hispano roots of New Mexico's history. Having not learned about this past either at home or in school, Chávez felt—and believed that those whom he called native New Mexicans did also—a certain historical vacuum or ambivalence at a time of increased Anglo-American influence in the post-World War II era.

Chávez approached the excavation of Hispanos' roots with a fervor and discipline that conveyed his religious commitment as a Franciscan. In a sense, he became a historical missionary. History, especially the role of the Hispano Church, would bring new spiritual and cultural nourishment to his people.

Chávez's historical pilgrimage became both a personal as well as a collective endeavor. Of this connection between the personal and the collective in his work, Father Thomas Steele has written concerning *My Penitente Land,* Fray Angélico's most autobiographical historical text, "Chávez's book embodies

Chávez's New Mexico, '*my* penitente land': his personally appropriated New Mexico, the New Mexico that formed him into the man he is, the New Mexico that is profoundly and vastly more *his* than it is anybody else's."[2] Chávez himself acknowledged his personal identification with the Hispano roots of New Mexico: "I myself was born when those first Spanish settlers were preparing to enter New Mexico, their land and mine. A goodly number of them are my own proven direct ancestors, some by several lines."[3]

If history was a way to understand one's own genealogy, it was also a way of providing a collective identity. For example, in his important work on tracing the origins of New Mexican Hispano families, Fray Angélico provided a sense not only of roots but perhaps more importantly of subjectivity—of being somebody. Chávez believed that Hispanos and non-Hispanos needed to know the Spanish-surname background of Hispano families as well as the place names that derived from Spanish names. *Origins of New Mexico Families: A Genealogy of the Spanish Colonial Period,* first published in 1954, represents a form of "collective biography" by its attention to the stories of the various Hispano family lines from the seventeenth century to the mid-nineteenth century. This includes families such as the Armijos, the Vigils, the Vargases, and, of course, the Chávezes. Fray Angélico, never fully accepting what Carey McWilliams called the "Spanish Fantasy," noted that while many of these initial families had migrated to New Mexico in hopes of achieving social status as hidalgos, most were of modest military and pastoral backgrounds: "good folks in the main, who were neither peons nor convicts."[4] But what particularly impressed Fray Angélico was how closely knit these kinships were. In effect, he saw colonial Hispano settlements as family or at least extended family.[5]

Part of Fray Angélico's search for personal and collective historical roots involved countering the view from Anglo-America of native New Mexicans, both Indians and Hispanos, as being the "other": of not being truly American, and of possessing a culture including religious practices that did not conform to an Anglo-American standard. Chávez opposed these biased and even racist opinions by stressing the deep roots of Hispanos in an area that became part of the United States.

Fray Angélico believed in an inclusive rather than an exclusive American history. Displaying what Herbert Eugene Bolton called the concept of "Greater America," Chávez, at the risk of uncritically examining the role of the Spanish conquering expeditions into New Mexico, nevertheless used these *entradas*— including that of Coronado in 1540—to emphasize the long-standing Hispanic presence in the region. This was looking at American history from a south-to-north perspective, opposing the standard narrative that American history begins with the thirteen original colonies. Chávez revised or attempted to revise this interpretation by integrating the Spanish colonies that antedated the first English settlements. In this version, Coronado is just as American as John Smith.

In seeking the historical roots of New Mexico from the perspective of religion, Fray Angélico further asserted the Hispanic character of the area by ascribing a sacredness to it. Like Chicano movement activists who linked the concept of Aztlán (the mythical pre-Columbian roots of the Southwest) to that of sacred space, Chávez interpreted Hispanic New Mexico in a similar vein. Comparing New Mexico to other parts of the United States, Fray Angélico wrote, "But the New Mexican landscape has something that they all lack. It is Holy Land." The Rio Grande in Chávez's narrative becomes the River Jordan.[6] Religion or sacredness permeated New Mexico.

Fray Angélico noted that many towns and geographic sites possessed religious names. In his work on New Mexican religious place names, he countered the tendency by Anglos to dehistoricize the landscape pertaining to the pre-American period. It is this religiosity or sacredness that he believed to be at the heart of New Mexico's early Hispanic past—religiosity that not only reinforced Fray Angélico's own personal devotion to the Church but also gave this history its special quality.

Through his research in early Church documents and in his impressive annotation of the archives of the Archdiocese of Santa Fe from 1678 to 1900, Chávez documented the origins of American history in New Mexico. He was saying that New Mexico and its native Hispano population possessed a history because they could document it. Here the role of the Church as the guardian of historical identity was crucial.

The religious nature of this history validated for Fray Angélico the Hispano experience. To him, religion was synonymous with ethnicity, at a time (the 1940s and 1950s) when it was not particularly acceptable to be "ethnic" or to assert in any oppositional manner one's ethnic identity, a time Daniel Bell has called the "Age of Consensus." This is not to say that Chávez was simply using religion to discuss ethnicity, but rather that for him religion and ethnicity in the case of New Mexico's colonial history were one and the same. "One can only feel the highest admiration for the majority of the padres," he concluded, "who kept the missions going in the face of either poverty and loneliness, and for the Hispanic folk who for generations had survived among perils and hardship that might have driven other people to desertion, if not extinction."[7]

In this search for roots, Fray Angélico clearly did not believe that the clock could be moved back. As with other native New Mexican writers there is in Chávez's writings a touch of nostalgia, but there is also a realistic awareness that well into the twentieth century many new changes had taken place. "We can't turn history back," he noted, "no matter how many efforts are now being made to remedy old injustices."[8] Indeed, it was precisely these transformations, such as the growing acculturation of Hispanos, that motivated Fray Angélico's search for history. He sensed a loss of historical identity and lamented it. Lack of identity disempowered Hispanos in a land that bore so much of their imprint. To empower Hispanos, Fray Angélico embarked on a crusade to regain this self-awareness. This was not nostalgia but a struggle to combat prejudice and the perceived loss of religious fervor among native New Mexicans. Historical consciousness, for Chávez, was the remedy for achieving equality and regaining one's soul.

III

A second major theme in Fray Angélico's historical writings concerns historical agency. That is, Mexican Americans, or in this case Hispanos, have not been merely victims of history but themselves have made history. Of course, in his work on the colonial Spanish missions and settlements Chávez was attesting to the agency of these ancestors. But the theme of agency is even better expressed in his volumes on the nineteenth century, in particular his texts on Padre Antonio José Martínez and Padre José Manuel Gallegos.

These works, which are also studies on leadership, were to a large degree a response to the racism expressed toward Hispanos in the American period of New Mexico. Early Anglo writers, such as W. W. H. Davis, Josiah Gregg, and Susan Shelby Magoffin, portrayed Hispanos as immoral, unscrupulous, and without honor or virtue. They particularly criticized them for their predilections for gambling, drinking, and immoral sexual behavior. This critique extended to the clergy, especially to key leaders such as Martínez and Gallegos. The general view of Martínez, for example, was of an immoral priest who was disloyal to the new American church hierarchy as well as to the United States. Perhaps the most influential impression of Martínez was Willa Cather's characterization of the Hispano priest in her classic *Death Comes for the Archbishop*. In her fictional account of events in New Mexico following the U.S. takeover, Cather set up Bishop Lamy, the new head of the Church in New Mexico, as the hero and Padre Martínez as the villain.

Such stereotypes of Hispanos, especially the clergy, disturbed Chávez. He saw these criticisms, which he felt continued to his own day, as inaccurate and harmful, causing much damage to ethnic relations and to Hispano self-image. Fray Angélico sought to revise such views. Unfortunately referring to Cather as a spinster, he nevertheless admired her talent as a writer but dismissed her as a historian by observing that her characterization of Padre Martínez was more legend than history. "Cather's version reflects the cynical view which had come down from the padre's foes," he proposed.[9] Cather, according to Chávez, was simply repeating the same biased views toward Martínez and other Hispano clergy that had been expressed in the 1850s with the arrival of the French priests such as Bishop Lamy and his right-hand man, Father Machebeuf.

Chávez believed that what was really involved in the ethnic tensions that resulted from the American takeover was that the newcomers lacked a knowledge of Hispano culture and an unwillingness to learn.[10] What Lamy, Machebeuf, Cather, and other later critics of Hispano culture did not understand, he felt, was that New Mexico, like the rest of Spanish America, had never been effectively influenced by the Reformation and the Counter-Reformation. These areas in the Americas were not part of the Puritan worldview that had affected the United States much more. Not aware of this, Anglo-Americans and other strangers to New Mexico unfairly attempted to impose their own "puritanical" views and values on a people and a culture that were less repressed about God and life.

Fray Angélico countered the new "Puritan history" or what he also called the "Aryan history" of the Anglo-American era by his revisionist studies of Padres Martínez and Gallegos. Besides their clerical duties, both priests participated in political activities before and after the U.S. conquest. Both were also excommunicated or defrocked by Bishop Lamy. Yet rather than seeing them as rogue priests, Chávez reinvented their images by portraying them in more complicated terms. Martínez and Gallegos represent not villains but leaders and heroes to the Hispano population. To Fray Angélico they stood as role models.

This is especially true of Padre Martínez. In the New Mexican priest, Chávez found a variety of admirable qualities. These include Martínez's political liberalism, which he took from his own esteem for Padre Hidalgo and the movement for Mexican independence. Martínez supported *los de abajo*—the underdogs—in his society, such as the often-repressed Penitente brotherhood, and the *santeros,* whom both the Mexican hierarchy and the later American one frowned upon. Chávez further championed Martínez for his enlightened educational views. Fray Angélico noted that Padre Martínez operated one of the early printing presses in New Mexico, and he used the press to publish both religious and educational texts, including the first books ever printed in New Mexico. Martínez was also a supporter of human rights and a humanist. Although a strong defender of Mexico's independence and of the new republic, Martínez, according to Chávez, gave greater weight to "the equal rights of all men without distinction under their Common creator."[11]

No doubt seeing much of himself in Martínez, Chávez likewise observed that Martínez was a conflicted individual with his own contradictions. Still, Fray Angélico revised the Cather-inspired view of Martínez as a disloyal priest and rebel by documenting that, despite his differences with the new French priests after the U.S. takeover, Martínez never repudiated Lamy's authority nor participated in rebellious action against American rule.[12]

At the same time, however, Padre Martínez, like Fray Angélico himself, believed in reinforcing a native New Mexican identity, especially in reaction to new and hostile forces after the American annexation. Chávez praised Martínez and Gallegos for "cherishing the Castilian pride of their own heritage."[13] It was Anglo-American racism, according to Chávez, that created the grounds for the invention of a Hispano ethnic identity as a form of self-protection. "But it was this Iberian proudful consciousness," he wrote of both Martínez and Gallegos, "which lay behind what some have called this stubbornness or recalcitrance when confronted later on with challenges which they considered unjust by their very nature."[14]

Padre Martínez, Fray Angélico concluded, was a "major genius in his own century as well as those before and after his time."[15] Denied their own heroic nature and their subjectivity in history in the American period, including in Chávez's own time, the Hispanos in New Mexico needed to know that they possessed a genealogy of leadership and agency and that it included the clergy. No doubt Fray Angélico believed that in his own way, through his writings and art, he was following in the footsteps of Martínez and Gallegos, who practiced, one might suggest, a form of nineteenth-century theology of liberation.

IV

The third major theme in Fray Angélico's historical writings concerns his stress on New Mexican Hispano regional identity. His research in colonial records had led him to the conclusion that despite military, commercial, and religious connections between New Mexico and the rest of New Spain, for the most part due to distance and hostile topography New Mexico remained isolated and out of the mainstream. This allowed a regional culture and identity to develop and to evolve over several centuries. It was this identity that Fray Angélico believed was being lost and confused.

Much of the cause for this threat to the native New Mexican's positive self-image was the result of a century of Anglo-American racism and denigration of the native customs. Rather than understanding the unique regional aspects of Hispano culture, most Anglos lumped this way of life under the category of "Mexican," thereby homogenizing the experience rather than appreciating the differentiation between New Mexican and Mexican ways of life. "For the English-speaking American," Fray Angélico observed, "it was then easy in the extreme to begin and continue making New Mexico more and more his own, and in his philistine image. Whatever was 'mexican,' as he termed the entire regional tradition . . . had no place in the new scheme of things."[16] Chávez abhorred what he termed "the Nordic notion of superman" that Anglo-Americans had introduced into New Mexico and that had marginalized, except for tourist purposes, Hispano culture and identity.[17]

This segregation had produced ambivalence and a loss of historical memory among Hispanos. Yet, as Fray Angélico noted, there was still enough of a way of life, of a way of looking at the world and at God that reminded Hispanos that they possessed a particular New Mexican identity. In his quasi-autobiographical *My Penitente Land,* Fray Angélico poignantly referred to both the ambivalence and the memory:

> This matter of antiquity, the very vagueness of it, played havoc with my young mind. I also remember asking my mother more than once why we were not exactly the same in speech and demeanor as the priest from Spain who was our assistant pastor at the time, and why we differed in the same way from a family from Mexico living up the street from us. She would flush with impatience—at her own inability to explain, I am sure— merely saying that our forebears had come from Spain a very long time ago. But she didn't know when or how. All this made the double puzzle of Penitentes and ancestral origins merge most confusedly inside my inquisitive young head.[18]

But it was still this sense that Hispanos had lived a certain history that drove Fray Angélico to rediscover it and to uphold it. This became part of his mission. He pursued what he called the "native soul."[19]

This soul, however, had suffered much in attempting to know itself. Indeed, for Chávez, one of the characteristics of being a native New Mexican was suffering and doing penance. Due to their isolation, their lack of material comforts, and the threats to their communities from the outside, Hispanos since the colonial era had been penitents, or Penitentes. Fray Angélico noted the evolution of certain of these brotherhoods, but suggested that in a spiritual sense all Hispanos were Penitentes.

Part of the Hispanos' penance, Fray Angélico suggested, was not being accepted as native to New Mexico and instead being compartmentalized as "Mexicans" by Anglos, implying that Hispanos were immigrants and foreigners. "And yet they do not wish to be identified as Mexicans," Chávez pointed out, "but correctly as long-time Americans by birth and nationality. Their not being accepted as such in the national picture of the United States has been part of their continuing penance. While being classified as Mexicans, which should bear no stigma at all, they do know, if more with the heart than with the head, that their own ancestry, language, and traditions are distinct from the Mexican."[20] Yet what helped Hispanos to protect their regional identity was the mountainous topography of New Mexico that sheltered them and their traditions. The "Spanish New Mexicans," he concluded, "know that they are not aliens, but natives of their very own landscape for almost four hundred years."[21]

What was distinctive about Hispanos, according to Chávez, was not so much racial as cultural. It was a way of life and a worldview that had evolved for centuries in relative isolation until the Anglo-American intervention as well as later increased immigration from Mexico. But more than anything, Fray Angélico stressed the importance of religion to the formation of a regional Hispano experience. For Chávez religion was Hispano identity. He did not necessarily mean institutionalized religion, since this had come largely under the control of non-Hispanics after the American annexation. Instead, Fray Angélico noted the continuities of popular or folk religious practices and confraternities, many of which could be traced to the colonial past. Here his work over the years in researching and writing about the veneration of La Conquistadora, the image of the Virgin Mary that had been used in the Reconquest of New Mexico in 1693 following the Pueblo Revolt of 1680, is particularly critical. Not only had his own family been involved in organizing the annual processions around La Conquistadora in Santa Fe, but Fray Angélico also observed the centrality of this devotion to maintaining a sense of community among Hispanos. La Conquistadora, whom he called "*paisana*," was both a religious symbol and an ethnic one. "Our ancestors have been witness to her glory," he wrote, "and she in turn bears witness to our parentage."[22]

Fray Angélico acknowledged that many efforts had been made by non-Hispano Catholics to eliminate or destroy popular Hispano religious traditions, including the Penitente brotherhoods, but they had all failed. For Chávez, it was these forms of religious practices more than anything else that kept alive the Hispano soul.

V

Besides stressing the contributions to Southwestern and American history by a remarkable writer and scholar, in my interpretation of Fray Angélico Chávez's

historical work I have also suggested that his texts represent a form of oppositional narrative. This opposition is based on countering racist and stereotypical
images of Hispanos in New Mexico and their marginalization in the region. By
rediscovering the long and rich historical roots of Hispanos, their leadership in
making history, and their development of a particular regional ethnic identity
heavily influenced by their religious practices, Fray Angélico sought not only to
combat prejudice but to provide testimony to his and his people's being and
self-worth. These contributions need to be recognized and his work integrated
by those of us who desire to revise American history in the hope of making this
country a more hospitable one for all who contribute to it.

NOTES

1. As quoted in Robert Huber, "Fray Angélico Chávez: 20th-Century Renaissance Man,"
New Mexico Magazine 48 (March–April 1970), p. 19.

2. See Father Thomas J. Steele's foreword to the 1993 edition of Fray Angélico Chávez, *My
Penitente Land* (Santa Fe: Museum of New Mexico Press, 1993), p. v.

3. Ibid., p. 5.

4. Chávez, *Origins of New Mexico Families: A Genealogy of the Spanish Colonial Period*
(1954; Santa Fe: William Gannon, 1975), p. xix.

5. Ibid.

6. Chávez, *My Penitente Land*, p. 28.

7. *The Missions of New Mexico, 1776, A Description by Fray Francisco Atanasio Domínguez
with Other Contemporary Documents*, translated by Elinor B. Adams and Fray Angélico
Chávez (Albuquerque: University of New Mexico Press, 1956), p. xviii. Also see Chávez,
"New Mexico Place-Names From Spanish Proper Names," *El Palacio* 56 (Dec. 1949), pp.
367–82; and Chávez, *Archives of the Archdiocese of Santa Fe, 1678–1900* (Washington, D.C.:
Academy of American Franciscan History, 1957).

8. Chávez, "Ruts of the Santa Fe Trail," *New Mexico Magazine* (July–Aug. 1972), p. 22.

9. Chávez, *But Time and Chance: The Story of Padre Martínez of Taos, 1793–1867* (Santa Fe:
Sunstone Press, 1981) p. 158; also see Chávez, *Très Macho—He Said: Padre Gallegos of Albuquerque, New Mexico's First Congressman* (Santa Fe: William Gannon, 1985), p. 37.

10. Chávez, "Doña Tules: Her Fame and Her Funeral," *El Palacio* 57 (Aug. 1950), pp. 230–
31.

11. Chávez, *But Time and Chance*, p. 51.

12. Ibid., p. 56.

13. Chávez, *Très Macho*, p. 2.

14. Ibid., p. 6.

15. Chávez, *But Time and Chance*, p. 160.

16. Chávez, *Penitente Land*, p. 254.

17. Ibid., p. 258.

18. Ibid., p. xi.

19. Ibid., p. 267.

20. Ibid., p. 266.

21. Ibid., p. 267.

22. Chávez, "La Conquistadora Is a Paisana," *El Palacio* 57 (Oct. 1950), p. 307. Also see Chávez, *La Conquistadora: The Autobiography of an Ancient Statue* (Paterson, N.J.: St. Anthony Guild Press, 1954).

CHAPTER THREE

LA CONQUISTADORA AS HISTORY AND FICTITIOUS AUTOBIOGRAPHY

LUIS LEAL
University of California, Santa Barbara

Fray Angélico Chávez's earliest interest as a writer was poetry. However, in the 1940s he began to publish history and historical fiction. In his documented study "La Conquistadora Is a Paisana," he wrote, "Three years ago, led by an irresistible fascination, I began to piece together a few known facts about La Conquistadora in an effort to separate fact from fiction."[1] Twenty years later (1970) he stated that he "took up history because it's there and makes my writing readable. There was a drama to the colonial life, and I have found its records."[2] His first historical monograph, "Nuestra Señora del Rosario, La Conquistadora," appeared in 1948 in the *New Mexico Historical Review,* and that same year it was revised and reprinted in book form by the Historical Society of New Mexico as *Our Lady of the Conquest.*[3] Six years later, under the title *La Conquistadora: The Autobiography of an Ancient Statue,* he transformed that documented history into a fictionalized autobiography of this most famous New Mexican statue of the Virgin Mary. In that book, instead of the author as a historian writing a biography, he lets the statue itself relate its life and adventures as if she were a real person. Here, Chávez's focus has changed. Instead of separating fact from fiction, which was his original aim when he took up history, he reverses the process and combines both discourses to produce a very original fictitious autobiography.

That La Conquistadora is the same statue brought to New Mexico by Fray Alonso de Benavides in 1625 is the thesis of Fray Angélico's 1948 monograph. Two years later he said, "I discovered seventeenth-century documents about La Conquistadora which supported the conclusions I had previously drawn."[4] During Fray Alonso's time the statue represented the Virgin of the Assumption, as stated by the author in his *Memorial* of 1630; it was much later that she became La Conquistadora. In Chávez's book of 1954, the statue says, "I have been in this country [the United States] for more than three hundred and twenty-five years."[5] In the chapter "Apaches, vaqueros del ganado de Síbola" of the *Memorial,* Benavides says, "*y habiendo sus Capitanes mayores oído decir que los españoles en la villa de Santa Fe tenían a la Madre de Dios, que era una imagen de bulto del Tránsito de la Virgen nuestra Señora que yo allí había llevado y estaba bien adornada en una capilla, vinieron a verla y le quedaron muy aficionados y le prometieron ser cristianos*" (. . . and their principal captains having heard that the Spaniards in the village of Santa Fe had the Mother of God, which was a statue of Our Lady the Virgin of the Assumption, which I had brought there and was very well dressed, in a niche, they came to see her and remained very devoted and promised to become Christians).[6]

The statue says she has been in New Mexico for 325 years. This number is apparently derived from Fray Alonso's *Memorial* of 1630, in which he states, "*Y el año pasado de 29 fue Dios servido que los redujésemos de paz*")(And last year, [16]29, God was served, for we were able to make peace with them [the Pueblo Indians]).[7] If 1629 is subtracted from 1954, the year the autobiography of the statue was published, the result is 325 years.

Fray Angélico's sources for the writing of his fictionalized autobiography, as listed in the book's "Bibliography and Historical Comment," are historical in nature.[8] And although all the historical references mentioned by the statue can be documented, the book is often classified as fiction. Alejandro Morales, in his doctoral dissertation, speaks of *La Conquistadora* as a novel.[9] This is true only in the context of the picaresque novel, which is essentially a fictitious auto-biography narrated by the protagonist, a *pícaro.* There are novels in which the narrator is a *pícara,* as in Francisco López Ubeda's *La pícara Justina* (1605), Alonso Jerónimo de Salas Barbadillo's *La hija de Celestina* (1612), and Alonso de Castillo Solórzano's *La niña de los embustes, Teresa de Manzanares* (1632). In Mexico, José Joaquín Fernández de Lizardi published *La Quijotita y su prima* in 1818, and in 1969 Elena Poniatowska her novel *Hasta no verte Jesús mío,* in which the protagonist, Jesusa Palancares, relates her life. The difference be-tween these novels and *La Conquistadora* is found not in the form but in the subject matter and the attitude of the narrator towards life, which is not pica-resque but historical and religious in nature. Other antecedents for wooden figures who talk and act are found in the popular puppet shows, an excellent example of which is the "Retablo de las maravillas" in Cervantes's *Don Quijote,* wherein the knight errant engages the puppets in combat.

The statue of the Virgin Mary brought to New Mexico by Fray Alonso in 1625 did not become a Conquistadora until much later in the century. It was first called, by Benavides, "Tránsito de la Virgen," a name translated by Fray Angélico as "Assumption of the Virgin." In his early book *Our Lady of the Conquest* he gives the following reasons to justify his translation: "I have used the word 'Assumption' for '*Tránsito*' in the originals [1630 and 1634 editions of the Benavides *Memorial*], which others have translated as the 'death' of the Virgin. Their translation is correct literally, but wrong liturgically. In employing the word 'Tránsito,' Fr. Benavides, by metonymy, was merely using one of the three ideas celebrated in the title and feast of the Assumption: The Death or Passing Away of Mary, her Assumption into Heaven, and her Coronation."[10] In *La Conquistadora* the statue says, "In the beginning I was 'Our Lady of the Assumption,' then for a short time 'The Immaculate Conception,' and finally 'Our Lady of the Rosary.' In these titles I was regarded by my people as Queen of New Mexico and of Santa Fe, but all the while, as with a beloved actress, I have been popularly known as 'La Conquistadora'" (p. 4). The statue also tells us the reason for her popular name: "My name for centuries has been 'La Conquistadora.' This is because I came to the Southwest with the Spanish pioneers who called themselves conquistadores" (p. 3). Historically, however, she was not called La Conquistadora until 1693, the year Diego de Vargas returned the statue to Santa Fe after his reconquest of the Pueblo Indians.

On August 10, 1680, the Pueblo Indians revolted and set siege to Santa Fe. In spite of a counterattack on August 20, for which the people "invoked my aid with special prayers the night before," they were forced to abandon the city and go south to El Paso. "I myself left Santa Fe clasped in the arms of a young housewife, who pressed her wet and trembling cheek to mine and wept as she trudged along with the rest. Her name was Josefa López Sambrano de Grijalva" (p. 59). The Reconquest of Santa Fe was begun by Don Diego de Vargas in 1692, and it was not until December 16,1693, that he triumphantly entered the city. Although the Reconquest started out under the banner of the Lady of the Remedies, he changed it to the Lady of the Conquest. On January 16, 1693, Vargas wrote to the viceroy in Mexico City, "It is my wish . . . that they should . . . build the church and holy temple, setting up in it before all else the patroness of the said kingdom and villa, who is the one that was saved from the fury of the savages, her title being Our Lady of the Conquest" (p. 75).

The fictitious aspect of the autobiography is found in its use of an old narrative technique, that of letting an inanimate object become the narrator. This technique is common in Latin American fiction. In 1930, for example, Francisco Rojas González, in Mexico, published *Historia de un frac,* in which the *frac* (full-dress coat) is the narrator, who tells about his life. In 1965 the Argentinean Marco Denevi published the short story "Apocalipsis," in which a machine is the narrator, a fact the reader doesn't know until the final phrase.

In *La Conquistadora* the wooden statue begins to speak about her life since she was carved in Spain from a piece of the trunk of a willow tree. The trip across the ocean to the city of Mexico, where she was brought by an unnamed person, is hardly recollected. She says, "I remember, later on, a journey over water—an ocean, or a lake, it does not matter. Next I found myself in a different land" (p. 6). In 1623 Fray Alonso saw her and decided to take her to New Mexico, as he had been appointed head of the missions there. His decision to take this statue and not another was based on two reasons, the statue's beauty and her small size:

> It was then that he first saw me and called me beautiful with his eyes. His heart decided at once that I would go with him to Santa Fe, and there reign in its parish church of the Assumption. Not only did my loveliness captivate Father Alonso, but my small self was just right, since it was impractical to haul large statues, in those early days, on a journey by oxcart that took at least three months over trackless mountains and deserts. And a man like Father Alonso had little trouble in getting my owner to part with me. (p. 9)

If she could not remember her trip across the ocean, her twelve-hundred-mile trip by oxcart from Mexico City to Santa Fe is told with numerous details, such as the places where they stopped (Tepeyac, Zacatecas, Durango, El Paso) and the people who accompanied them, such as the new governor of New Mexico, don Francisco Sotelo, and Captain Francisco Gómez, a Portuguese soldier (an ancestor of Fray Angélico), and many others. She describes the landscape, the desert, the climate, and other elements. Well packed in a wooden crate, she tells the story of the Virgin of Guadalupe, about whom she says, talking directly to the reader, "Most of you already know about the heavenly painting of Our Lady of Guadalupe. It could be that someone might suspect that I, as a woman, could be jealous of a rival representation of the Mother of God. I am only jesting, of course" (pp.10–11). Similar statements demonstrate her human nature, a characteristic of the statue very well developed by Fray Angélico. The historical source of the story of the Virgin of Guadalupe is the *Historia de la Virgen de Guadalupe,* published in Mexico City in 1897 by an anonymous Jesuit. Conscious of the fact that this is a very common story, the author has the statue say, again talking to the reader, "If I have bored you by recounting this well-known happening in its every detail, I myself have greatly enjoyed retelling it" (p. 19).

Technically, the statue could only be remembering the story through interior monologue, since she is enclosed in a strong case nailed inside a sturdy wooden box. This observation can be made about all the other references to reality outside the box during the trip. Readers, of course, accept the omniscient nature of the statue, since from the beginning, as in all fables, they have suspended their disbelief in admitting that the statue can talk.

The fictitious element in this book—letting a wooden statue be the narrator—has the function of an esthetic frame, in which a novelistic discourse is used in order to make the history of New Mexico, from the early seventeenth century to the middle of the nineteenth, as interesting as possible. There is no question that Fray Angélico's aim is to retell that history, as he did in his earlier works about La Conquistadora. In the fictitious autobiography he makes use of all the historical sources he used before, beginning with the two versions of Fray Alonso de Benavides's *Memoriales* (1630, 1634) as well as information about Fray Alonso himself. The statue says,

> Fray Alonso de Benavides left us when the supply ox train departed for New Spain in the fall of 1629. The following year he wrote a *Memorial* describing the missions of New Mexico, their great problems and greater possibilities. This was presented [by Fray Juan de Santander] to the King of Spain, was printed in Madrid, and soon was being translated and published in various countries of Europe. Three years later he wrote a revision of it at the request of Pope Urban VIII. In both works, Fray Alonso makes special mention of me" (p. 30).

The statue's main interests, when she is not talking about herself, are history, religion, and the biography of Fray Angélico's ancestors, of whom there is a genealogical tree at the beginning of the book. The statue is very skillful about characterizing herself and is not jealous, as she says, of other representations of the Mother of God. Besides the Mexican Virgin of Guadalupe, whom she praises, she relates the lives of the Spanish Virgin of Guadalupe, Our Lady of the Remedies, Our Lady of Light, and Our Lady of Toledo. The Spanish Virgin of Guadalupe has a long history. The medium is the same as that of La Conquistadora: "It is a seated figure of wood, about my own height, representing Mary with her Child on her left arm." She appeared during the thirteenth century to a peasant of Cáceres, Extremadura, who was looking for a stray cow and told him to dig at the spot where they would find her image and build there a shrine for her. "In the year 1340 this Alfonso [Alfonso XI] won a great victory over Albohacen, the ruler of Morocco, after imploring the help of Our Lady of Guadalupe" (p. 42).

In the New World, the first Conquistadora was not New Mexico's Lady of the Assumption but the Lady of Remedies, brought by Hernán Cortés to

Mexico in 1519. The New Mexico statuette recognizes this fact: "the first Conquistadora is a small statue of Our Lady of the Angels, known also afterward as Our Lady of Remedies, which Cortés had with him in the conquest of Mexico City" (p. 51).

When La Conquistadora speaks about herself, she gives emphasis to her feminine traits. She does not mind being compared with actresses, for, "like one, I have played the part of Mary in different glorious roles." She is old, but "a lady, even a wooden one, will not tell her exact age" (p. 4). When Father Domínguez speaks of her as being about a yard tall, very old, recently retouched, and wearing a wig, she becomes indignant: "He somehow insulted me . . . was rather cruel in his veracity" (p. 105). She does not hide the fact that she likes men: "I myself liked the captain, too, knowing that he also would love me . . ." (p. 24).

La Conquistadora is also tolerant. She defends Francisco Gómez Robledo, the son of Francisco Gómez and Ana Robledo, who is accused of Judaism, for his sons were supposed to have tails. Her knowledge of anatomy is revealed when she explains the reason people think Gómez's sons have tails: "The fact is that one of the sons (some said Juan, others said Francisco) had an abnormal coccyx. . . . This tiny bone at the end of the spine stuck out instead of curling inward and out of sight under the skin, as with most people" (p. 37). Of the racial conflict with the Indians she says, "a passion blinder even than that of the flesh, it seems, is that of race" (p. 73).

Most of the text of La Conquistadora is taken up with the history of New Mexico: the exploration and founding of the villages by Juan de Oñate in 1598; the arrival and departure of Fray Alonso de Benavides and Governor Sotero; the short period of Flores as governor and his appointment of Francisco Gómez as acting governor; the 1680 uprising of the Pueblo Indians and the abandonment of Santa Fe by governor Otermin; the Reconquest of Santa Fe by Don Diego de Vargas in 1693 and his imprisonment by Governor Pedro Cuervo in 1697, and Vargas's campaign against the Pueblo Indians in 1706; the defeat of the Utes and Comanches by acting Governor Valverde; the long period (1717–65) of Bernardino de Sena ("born in the Valley of Mexico, not far from the shrine of Guadalupe") as *mayordomo* of the statue's confraternity; the governments of other obscure rulers until 1821, when New Mexico is "no longer a Kingdom but a poor forgotten frontier province" (p. 114); the Mexican governors and the conquest of New Mexico by General Kearny; and the arrival of Bishop Lamy in 1851.

The other important elements in the book are the references to Fray Angélico's ancestors, beginning with Captain Francisco Gómez and his wife, Ana Robledo. Right after the title, he presents a genealogical tree of his family from the early seventeenth century to the time the book was published. Throughout the narrative, these persons appear associated with the activities of La Conquistadora. The founder of the family, Captain Gómez, was Portuguese, "born in a suburb of Lisbon [Coina, near Lisbon], and after both his parents died, was reared" by a half-brother. He was brought to Mexico by a brother of Juan de Oñate and then came to New Mexico, where he was given an *encomienda* (p. 23). Soon he was promoted to *sargento mayor* and became one of the most powerful men in New Mexico. His wife, Ana Robledo, born in San Gabriel, New Mexico, in 1600, was twenty-five years old when La Conquistadora came to Santa Fe. Ana married Francisco Gómez in that city and had several children, among them Francisco Gómez Robledo, who was later accused of Judaism by the Inquisition, as was his father. La Conquistadora says about the family, "Ana Robledo lived on for many years, and some of her children also, to be further knitted into my life's story" (p. 37).

In his 1950 article Fray Angélico included a brief list of his direct ancestors. "I will be brief," he says, "by enumerating them in handy Biblical fashion: Francisco Gómez and Ana Robledo begat Andrés Gómez Robledo . . . Romualdo Roybal, who begat María Nicolasa Roybal (my mother)." He continues, "This personal genealogy is not proffered here as a claim to any social superiority. In my opinion, the chief virtue of genealogies lies in the invaluable aid that they give to historical and social studies, and not in the vain pretensions for which genealogies are employed everywhere. By simply showing my own direct connection with the original and subsequent Conquistadora devotees I am also demonstrating how all native New Mexicans have been honoring their Queen."[11] From the perspective of La Conquistadora, this interest in genealogy has a different source: "At this particular period my people had become strongly aware of their ancestry, perhaps because there was not much else to boast about" (p. 50).

The autobiography ends with an epilogue in which La Conquistadora invites the reader to visit her in the Cathedral of Saint Francis of Assisi. She then goes on to describe her several dresses, all of them fashioned after those of an ancient Spanish queen. The nature of this most human statue is revealed when she says, "Of course, I know that I myself am not immortal. The day will come when I shall join the rest of the willow by being burned to ashes" (p. 131). Thus, the image of the willow that appears at the beginning of the autobiography, when the statue relates her birth, reappears at the end of the book, giving this most interesting fictitious autobiography an artistic narrative frame, a frame worthy of the painting of this most famous statue.

Often, fiction and history blend to create a new dimension. In *La Conquistadora* historical facts are intermingled with the statue's personal observations to give the narrative verisimilitude. When Don Diego de Vargas arrived in El Paso in 1691 (a historical fact about a real person), the statue adds, "He, too, fell in love with me" (a fictitious statement). Like a medieval lady, she has her knights, although they are not wooden but real: "My chief knight at this period was Don Juan Páez Hurtado" (p. 89). "But to me these particular [historical] people were the salt of the earth. Were it not for them I would not be known; perhaps I would not even exist today with a story to tell" (p. 93).

NOTES

1. Fray Angélico Chávez, "La Conquistadora Is a Paisana," *El Palacio* 57 (Oct. 1950), p. 305.

2. Clark Colahan, "Fray Angélico Chávez," in *Dictionary of Literary Biography*, edited by Francisco A. Lomelí and Carl R. Shirley (Detroit: Gale Research, 1989), pp. 86–90.

3. Fray Angélico Chávez, "Nuestra Señora del Rosario, La Conquistadora," *New Mexico Historical Review* 23 (April–July 1948), pp. 94–128, 177–216. Revised and reprinted as *Our Lady of the Conquest* (Santa Fe: Historical Society of New Mexico, 1948).

4. Chávez, "La Conquistadora Is a Paisana," p. 305.

5. Fray Angélico Chávez, *La Conquistadora: The Autobiography of an Ancient Statue* (Paterson, N.J.: St. Anthony Guild Press, 1954), p. 3. Subsequent quotations from this book are from this edition.

6. Fray Alonso de Benavides, *Memorial que Fr. Juan de Santander . . . presenta a . . . don Felipe Cuarto Nuestro Señor. Hecho por el padre Fray Alonso de Benavides 1630* (Mexico City: Museo Nacional de Mexico, 1899), p. 45.

7. Ibid., p. 23.

8. Chávez, *La Conquistadora: The Autobiography of an Ancient Statue*, pp. 133–34.

9. Alejandro Morales, "Visión panorámica de la literatura mexicoamericana hasta el boom de 1966," Ph.D. dissertation, Rutgers University, 1975, pp. 265–66.

10. Fray Angélico Chávez, *Our Lady of the Conquest*, p. 34 n46.

11. Chávez, "La Conquistadora Is a Paisana," pp. 306–7.

PART 2

CULTURE OF THE WORD AND IMAGE

CHAPTER FOUR

WONDERS AND TRUTHS:
The Short Stories of Fray Angélico Chávez

THOMAS J. STEELE, S.J.
Regis University, Denver

Scientists think in cause-and-effect sequences; and in history, one of the social sciences, Fray Angélico constructed and managed strings of cause and effect with the best of them. But he was also adept—I would say, even more talented and even more adept—at the sorts of human endeavors that proceed by patterns. Poetry is the arrangement of patterns in spoken language. The visual arts are arrangements of analogous patterns in space.

All his religious life, Father Chávez bore the name of a friar-artist of the early Renaissance, Blessed Fra Angelico of Fiesole, a holy Dominican. Moreover, our Fray Angélico wrote his 1933 bachelor's thesis on religious art. Titled "Painting, Personality, and Franciscan Ideals," the long essay showed how an appreciation for good sacred art could enhance the whole of a Franciscan lay brother's or priest's character.[1] Reality, for Fray Angélico, is very incarnational and sacramental: the spiritual and even the divine can be embodied in matter, and therefore the world of nature and even more so the world of sacred art serve the perceptive mind as clues to and bearers of the spiritual and the divine.

However important art theory may be, the practice of art is more important yet, and in 1940 Ina Sizer Cassidy profiled Angélico in her monthly column in *New Mexico Magazine* for his Peña Blanca murals of the Stations of the Cross, now unfortunately destroyed in the collapse of the church several years ago. Cassidy commented that Father Chávez "makes this sacred history a story of NOW" by using the likenesses of parishioners to depict the persons present at Christ's passion, death, and burial.[2] Though history and geography tell us that we are far removed in time and space from the sacred event, the sacred arts—the liturgy above all—make the sacred event present to us and make us present to it.

Fray Angélico's tales of New Mexico, those in his own slender volumes *New Mexico Triptych* and *From an Altar Screen* as well as those in Genaro Padilla's book of selections,[3] show the same trait of interchangeableness and inter-penetration between image and archetype, between present and past, between lesser self and Greater Other Self, that Ina Sizer Cassidy correctly perceived.

A word about this. Martin Buber's classic *I and Thou* suggests that there is a way in which an artifact participates in personhood, that a proper aesthetic contemplation of a painting is not just an I-it relationship but is truly (though in a limited manner) an interpersonal relationship, an I-Thou relationship.[4] Buber was thinking of the way in which a post-Renaissance artist—Raphael, say, or Rembrandt; Goya or Gauguin; Picasso or Pletka—is present to the viewer. But if we turn away from Renaissance art and turn to the medieval religious art of Europe, or even better, to the medieval religious folk art of eighteenth- and nineteenth-century New Mexico, the *santos,* we will find that the person in whom the painting or statue participates is not the artist, for true folk artists have always been self-effacing. It is instead the person of the subject—the archetype, the Greater Other Self—that the viewer becomes aware of when he or she prays before the *santo*: the painting on a pine panel, the statue of cottonwood root gessoed and polychromed. San José Patriarca is *here* for me; his sacred history is a story of NOW. As a philosopher might put it, the saint in heaven and the image of the saint are "not adequately distinct."

Greek Orthodox theologians said this sort of thing over and over as they tried to defeat the heresy of iconoclasm. Here's a sample of their thinking: "The imitative icon has no personhood of its own, but it brings with it the person of the archetype whose image it is. . . . When an icon represents any subject, it displays not the nature but the person. . . . If the shadow of a body never exists apart from the body but is always joined to it even when [the shadow] is unseen, neither can the icon of Christ be separated from him. . . . Christ himself is visible in his icon, which has its being in him."[5] Plainly, we find ourselves here in a Platonic world, a world of archetypes and participation where the holy persons take the place of Plato's subsistent Ideas.

In *My Penitente Land,* Father Chávez associates the *santos* with the earliest Romanesque art of Spain, which derived in turn from the Byzantine icons.[6] In his foreword to José Edmundo Espinosa's *Saints in the Valleys,* Fray Angélico explicitly stated that the *santos* possessed a sort of personal being because of their spirituality,[7] and it is exactly personhood—the personal, spiritual being of the saint in heaven—that asserts itself so dramatically at the most crucial moment in many of Fray Angélico's short stories about the traditional Hispanic people of New Mexico.

Latin American magical realism began in the field of art and spread into

Latin American literature in the 1950s and 1960s, long after Chávez had written his stories. Perhaps someone could make a case that he was, with José de la Cuadra, a grandfather of the movement in literature, but I think Chávez's stories belong mainly to the tradition of Anglo-American romanticism. The English background would include Walpole, Wordsworth, and Coleridge. The American might include touches of sentimental O. Henry realism, suitably rusticated to fit into the New Mexican countryside. There may also be faint echoes of Poe—let's say his "Oval Portrait." But the literary tradition I have in mind is best exemplified by any romance of Nathaniel Hawthorne, with its "latitude, both as to its fashion and material." The writer, Hawthorne goes on to say in the preface to *The House of the Seven Gables,* "may so manage his atmospherical medium as to bring out or mellow the lights and deepen and enrich the shadows of the picture. He will be wise [however] to mingle the Marvellous rather as a slight, delicate, and evanescent flavor than as any portion of the actual substance of the dish offered to the Public. He can hardly be said, however, to commit a literary crime, even if he disregard this caution."[8] Chávez committed no crime, but he certainly added more than a mere evanescent flavor of the marvelous. Miracles are the meat and potatoes of many of his stories. I find three sorts of marvelous, miraculous things that occur:

1. *A* santo—*a religious statue or painting—comes to life:* In the story "The Angel's New Wings," when Nabor the old *santero* pegs the second wing into place, the Christmas angel flies out of his hand, or seems to; at any rate, for the purposes of reading the story, the reader suspends disbelief and assumes that not only the angel but all the other figures of his crib scene come to life,—at least for Nabor. In "The Lean Years," a statue of San José Patriarca comes to life. In "Wake for Don Corsinio," the title character's dead wife Bárbara and the panel painting of Santa Bárbara both come to life, join into a single apparition, and speak to Corsinio.

2. *An otherworldly personage appears on earth, or at least clearly intervenes in human affairs:* During the Holy Week processions of northern New Mexico, Christ appears three times carrying his cross in the story "The Penitente Thief." The main character, Lucero, like the Good Thief in Luke's Gospel, responds well to the series of appearances, whereas the Bad-Thief character Maldonado, a gambler, politician, and lawyer, responds badly and comes eternally to no good end. Along the same line, in "The Tesuque Pony Express," Saint Anthony of Padua restores some lost money. In "The Ardent Commandant," the Devil himself takes the form of a dashing military officer. In yet another story, the soul of a newly dead child stops the town fiddler's donkey and makes him return to play his violin at the wake. In "The Bell That Sang

Again," Santa Ysabel, the mother of John the Baptist, appears to the young widow Ysabel and comforts her.

3. *A scriptural personage or a* santo *is assimilated to the pattern of a New Mexican in the story, or vice-versa*: Santa Ysabel, in "The Bell That Sang Again," becomes a New Mexican *anciana*, wearing a *rebozo*, smoking a hand-rolled cigarette, and dispensing wisdom to her young namesake. In "The Hunchback Madonna," the Lady of Guadalupe that a New Mexican *santero* paints strongly resembles the holy old hunchbacked woman so devoted to La Morenita. In "A Desert Idyll," both the risen Christ and the Christ Child who appeared in Saint Anthony of Padua's arms during a thirteenth-century apparition become identical with the consecrated host—the Eucharist—carried by a twentieth-century Franciscan missionary; and thus a dying Navajo woman is reconciled to her Maker.

In "The Bell That Sang Again," young Ysabel becomes Santa Ysabel when the babe in her womb quickens. The unfaithful woman in "Black Ewe" becomes the sole lamb of a poor man of which Nathan the prophet tells philandering David in Second Samuel. In "The Colonel and the Santo," a man who dies in the South Pacific during World War II becomes San Acacio, his patron saint, depicted in a panel painting in his mother's New Mexican home. And especially, in "The Ardent Commandant," the heroine's dead mother and father, her three dead husbands, her satanic tempter, the Blessed Virgin who rescues her, and she herself are all equated to images on the Castrense altar screen:

> Starting down from the rounded peak of the reredos, where the Eternal Father . . . blessed everything below, Doña Casilda prayed for her father.
>
> Beneath was the Madonna and Child, Our Lady of Valvanera, seated in the hollow of an ancient oak tree in her forest shrine in Navarre. . . . To her Casilda commended the saintly soul of her mother.
>
> Below this was the panel of Santiago the Apostle, who converted Spain; he was on horseback striving with raised sword for the Spanish armies against the Moors. In panels on either side of his were San José, patron of a happy death because he died in the arms of Jesus, and San Juan Nepomuceno. . . . To these three she [had] learned with the tragic years to entrust the souls of her three martyred soldier-husbands—and strange that their names should have been Santiago, José, and Juan.
>
> But to Casilda the most beautiful of all was the large oil painting of Nuestra Señora de la Luz, enthroned in the center of the reredos. . . . Our Lady of Light wore a white gown and flowing blue mantle, holding her Infant on her left arm, and with the other hand rescuing a young man from the gaping maw of an infernal monster. . . . But it seemed to Casilda that

the youth being helped didn't seem to care much whether he was saved or not. The artist had given him a blank look. Maybe he was stupid about such things, like so many people.[9]

And let me add: like Doña Casilda herself, who must be saved from the "gaping maw" of her infernal suitor.

In summary, what are the "ground rules" of the world that Fray Angélico Chávez has created for us in his short stories? First of all, things happen in Fray Angélico's tales not because effects follow from efficient causality but instead because archetypal exemplars are forever valid: the divinely given patterns of life will assert themselves as long as human life endures. Next, holy personages are by definition powerful, as Rudolf Otto made clear in his classic study *The Idea of the Holy*.[10] Since they are good, their power is power for life. Their power enables them to change their locations and their appearances, to come alive on earth in statues and paintings of themselves, to transform other persons—in Fray Angélico's stories, to convert them to good, reclaim them for their God, return them to themselves. And finally, traditional New Mexico did not think that the natural and supernatural orders, the realm of natural law and the realm of miracle, were identical; but the line between them, which had been so clear in the Reformation and Counter-Reformation theologies of Europe, certainly got blurred. The normal and the miraculous differed only as the usual and the slightly unusual, and they were expected to interpenetrate quite often. God and His saints were familiar—they were members of the family—in eighteenth- and nineteenth-century New Mexico.[11] This world in which saints appear, *santos* come alive, and miracles happen still lives for us, and will live forever, in the tales of Fray Angélico Chávez.

NOTES

1. Fray Angélico Chávez, O.F.M., "Painting, Personality and Franciscan Ideals," bachelor's thesis, Duns Scotus College, Detroit, 1933.

2. Ina Sizer Cassidy, "Fray Angélico Chávez," *New Mexico Magazine* 18 :3 (March 1940), pp. 27, 46.

3. *New Mexico Triptych* (Paterson: St. Anthony Guild Press, 1940); *From an Altar Screen* (New York: Farrar, Straus and Cudahy, 1957); Genaro M. Padilla, ed., *The Short Stories of Fray Angélico Chávez* (Albuquerque: University of New Mexico Press, 1987), especially pp. 117–29.

4. Martin Buber, *I and Thou* (New York: Charles Scribner's Sons, 1958), pp. 7–10, 33, 41; Buber, *Between Man and Man* (New York: Macmillan, 1965), pp. 15, 25–26; see also Mau-

rice S. Friedman, *Martin Buber: The Life of Dialogue* (New York: Harper and Brothers, 1960), pp. 166–73.

5. Euthymios Zigabenos, *Panoplia Dogmatica,* Section XXII (Against Iconoclasm), chapters 5, 7, 20, 22; from *Patrologium Graecum* 130, columns 1163–74, my translation.

6. *My Penitente Land,* foreword by Thomas J. Steele, S.J. (Santa Fe: Museum of New Mexico Press, 1993), p. 142.

7. Chávez, foreword to José Edmundo Espinosa, *Saints in the Valleys* (Albuquerque: University of New Mexico Press, 1960), pp. ix–x.

8. Nathaniel Hawthorne, Preface to *The House of the Seven Gables* (1852).

9. *From an Altar Screen,* pp. 42–43. The altar screen that appears in the story, set about 1790–92, may still be seen in actual historical and historic reality in the Church of Cristo Rey on Canyon Road in Santa Fe, constructed to showcase it in 1939–40.

10. Rudolf Otto, *The Idea of the Holy* (London: Oxford University Press, 1958). The Ernest Baughman Archive (# 317) at the Center for Southwest Research of the University of New Mexico (box 1, folder 108) includes a tale titled "The Santo Who Came to Life": "In a penitente church, a santo came to life. When a penitente before her tried to touch her, she struck him and he fell at her feet and died. When they looked up at her, she was crying tears of blood for having killed a man. This supposedly took place around Cañones." Compare the episode in 2 Samuel 6:6–7 when the oxen drawing the cart that held the Ark of the Covenant stumbled and Uzzah, not a priest, put his hand out to steady it and was struck dead. Holiness was power long before it had anything to do with moral goodness. Cf. also Navajo figures such as Holy Young Man.

11. Thomas J. Steele, S.J., *Santos and Saints* (Santa Fe: Ancient City Press, 1994), p. 7.

CHAPTER FIVE

ICONICITY AND NARRATIVE IN THE WORK OF FRAY ANGÉLICO CHÁVEZ:

Toward the Harmonious Imagetext

ELLEN MCCRACKEN
University of California, Santa Barbara

It should come as no surprise that New Mexico's foremost man of letters in the twentieth century frequently joins visual and verbal culture in his work. When nineteen-year-old Manuel Chávez began his new life as a Franciscan friar on August 15, 1929, he had already published poetry and displayed artistic talent; "Frater Angelico," the name he was given at the start of his new religious life, were words strongly imbued with the visual—the life and artistic production of the fifteenth-century Dominican painter Fra Angelico da Fiesole. What might surprise some, however, is the harmonious, noncompetitive relationship between the verbal and the visual in Fray Angélico Chávez's vast cultural production of painting, poetry, fiction, journalism, genealogy, philology, and revisionist history. Cultural theorists frequently perceive a dichotomous and oppositional relationship between the verbal and the visual, but in Fray Angélico's work the two are collaborative strategies linked by a common compelling impulse to narrate.

For Fray Angélico the verbal and the visual are elements of a continuum in which "strong" forms of one or the other predominate at either end, and numerous intermediary, composite works fill in the center positions. His cultural production of nearly seven decades moves beyond the neat borders between print and visual culture to include visual and "textual" material practices and artifacts not usually within the purview of literary and art criticism. Here I propose an integrative view of this diverse cultural production, focusing on the imbrication of the visual and verbal at several locations on the continuum. In the first category, language strives to represent the visual; at the opposite end, pictorial narrative is the predominant strategy; and in the center, Fray Angélico creates composite, intermediate texts that might be termed "imagetexts," following W. J. T. Mitchell's distinctions.[1]

VISIBLE LANGUAGE: THE ICONOLOGY OF THE TEXT

At the strongly verbal end of Fray Angélico's cultural production are three types of texts: those published with no accompanying visual images, those that Fray Angélico writes as if they would appear with only inadequate visual images or none at all, and the subsections of composite works in which the verbal text predominates. Even at this verbal end of the continuum, however, the visual plays a pivotal role.

In a prose piece written for his high-school seminary publication, the *Brown and White,* seventeen-year-old Manuel Chávez invites readers to join him in envisioning the beautiful seminary grounds as if from an airplane. Creating a species of illuminated letter with his verbal description of the scene, Chávez compares the grounds to a "vast, beautifully decorated flag" in which the yellow seminary building stands in the center "like a huge golden letter 'E,' as if suggesting the motto 'Excelsior.' The green woods encircling this raised monogram would form a holly-like wreath, from the verdant hues of which the red-roofed dwellings would shine out with the red of ripe, luscious berries. The private roads and pathways, winding through and around it, like so many white and silver ribbons, would gently break the green monotony."[2] Chávez imagines the turning roads to be "glistening streams," Springdale Pike to be the banner's white flagpole, and a curved road to the left to represent the waving movement of the imagined flag. This alternate visual encoding of the seminary grounds recalls Shklovsky's concept of the estrangement device whereby art renders the ordinary extraordinary. Chávez's movement between visual and verbal motifs in this entirely verbal text points to the harmonious, nonconflictive relationship he perceives between the two modes of expression.

In the "Prelude" to his 1960 novel *The Lady from Toledo,*[3] a section of a composite text in which the verbal predominates, Fray Angélico includes much visual description and important visual metaphors based on the motif of color. The revisionist history he will narrate in the rest of the book will use elements of popular religious legend to add "color" to "the black-and-white sketches [of the Pueblo Revolt of 1680] left by governors and captains"; secondly, his fictional intuitions in the novel will function as the missing third plate of the color printing process; and finally, he argues, the fictional lives he presents are like the colored patches of clothing and skin left by the culturally and racially diverse "little folk" of seventeenth-century New Mexico, which he will piece together in the revisionist narrative to follow.[4] By implication, he expects that the words he employs will "add color" to his own black-and-white drawings and the photo at the end, not vice-versa, as is usually assumed to be the case in illustrated texts.

In "New Mexico's Real Romeo and Juliet,"[5] a text written as if there would be no adequate visual accompaniment, Fray Angélico frequently strives to evoke the visual. Here he writes history as a prose play, with introductory notes, three acts, and an epilogue. "The very location lights up like a stage," he notes, urging readers to use his verbal description to "picture the Santa Fe plaza as it was [in the summer of 1733]" (p. 13). Throughout, he uses ekphrasis, the verbal attempt to portray the visual, in the mode in which Mitchell has configured it—a triangular relation between the visual object, the text, and the reader:

> The next scene is easy to imagine on that August 10th of 1733. The first church of Albuquerque was smaller than Santa Fe's own *parroquia*. Its plain front had no towers, and it faced eastward toward the majestic Sandía Mountains.
>
> Imagine the view from its bare front graveyard across the plaza—without the present trees and gazebo. . . . Now let us go inside the church. Father Montaño, still in his red vestments, stands waiting at the altar, while Aunt Josefa and a happy Francisca, standing to one side, also turn their expectant faces to the front entrance. (p. 45)

Fray Angélico's urge to narrate history to contemporary readers is intimately connected to his desire to make them see that which is no longer visually present. Thus, even when he works at the strongly verbal end of the cultural continuum, he relies on several varieties of visual language.

Many of his hundreds of poems similarly strive for ekphrasis, transcending what a practitioner of both the verbal and visual arts might perceive to be the limitations of nonillustrated publication venues. "The Angelus," for example, first published in 1930, when Chávez was a twenty-year-old seminarian, explicitly invokes Millet's painting, urging us to see key, although selected, elements of what Millet himself has seen. Inspired by his own contemporary vision of the late-nineteenth-century painting and attempting to compensate for the limitations of visual art, Fray Angélico adds the element of sound to Millet's visual imagery, engaging in rich synaesthesia: "A fading sky and steeple dim / Blend in audible harmony. . . . That painted peal on painted air, / That tinted tone. / The shades of night erase the sound. . . ."[6] Ingeniously, he has used the verbal to expand and compensate for the nonauditory nature of the painting, urging us to both hear and see the images evoked in a painting not visually present on the page.

In the playful 1971 poem "El Santo Closs,"[7] published with an only remotely related photograph, Chávez employs ekphrasis to move readers between two visual images—one, of the fourth-century bishop Saint Nicholas, and the other, of his Anglicized reconfiguration, Santa Claus. In this cultural "unfrocking," as Fray Angélico terms it, the key visual signifiers of the bishop's traditional image are transformed into peculiarly Anglo-American substitutions: within the vestimentary code, the "birette" becomes a cap, the "mozette" an overcoat, the red soutane a "trousered fur-lined suit," and silken buskins, Texas leather boots. But this visual history lesson also focuses on language, as Fray Angélico playfully explains the historical transformations of the linguistic code: where the Anglos "feminized" and abbreviated the saint's name, Spanish-speaking New Mexicans recapture the original gender as they incorporate the loan word from English as "El Santo Closs." Emphasizing the visual once again at the end of the poem, Fray Angélico sides with historical change and modernity, rejecting the bishop's "staid" religious attire in favor of the contemporary "heretical" garb Americans have come to love. The visual and verbal function cooperatively to remind readers of history no longer visually accessible; even when working within a primarily verbal medium, Chávez intertwines the verbal and visual to make readers know through seeing.

MATERIAL VISUAL CULTURE

At what might be termed the weakly verbal or, more positively, the strongly visual end of the continuum of Fray Angélico's cultural production is a varied set of artifacts that encourage historical remembrance. Here Chávez preserves, enhances, and visually narrates the history of New Mexico, frequently encoding ordinary people into the larger historical narrative. The work of restoring and renovating churches, painting large-scale interior and exterior murals, revitalizing religious ritual practices, and designing vestments, book seals, altar screens, doors, and monuments reveals Fray Angélico's sense of the centrality of public visual expression to the history and spirituality of New Mexico.

These public artifacts grew from Chávez's early artwork in the seminary. *Burros* (see frontispiece), a rustic painting of a New Mexico landscape, now housed in the Franciscan archives in Cincinnati, depicts a young burro suckling its mother, its tail resting gently down in contrast to the mother's tail in motion. Blues and greens predominate in the hillside behind, with a forest further back. The colors of the brown and yellow field in the foreground extend to the hill in the distance, and a sense of peace predominates. Through the painting, the young Chávez brings the visual presence of the remote rural landscape of New Mexico to the Cincinnati seminary, much as he would later make images of New Mexico's remote history visually present to twentieth-century New Mexicans.[8]

Unable to make the long trip home for holidays while studying in Cincinnati, Chávez was frequently invited to the family home of the rector of the seminary, Father Floribert Blank, in Batesville, Indiana. On the occasion of the eightieth birthday of Fr. Floribert's father, Chávez painted a gift for him—an image of Mr. Blank's cabin in the woods near Batesville, with smoke coming from the chimney in the form of the number 80.[9] This unique birthday gift points to Fray Angélico's early appreciation of history: Fr. Floribert's father had been one of the early settlers of the Batesville area, and the cabin represented his connection to the history of that place; the eighty years of his life, highlighted by the numerical configuration of the chimney smoke, joined the other key image of the cabin to link him to the history of the Midwest.

As a high-school student, Chávez received permission to paint a mural of Saint Francis feeding the birds on a white wall in the newly built seminary. In a quite different vein, he exhibited his characteristic impishness when allowed in 1928 to repaint the portrait of Saint Anthony preaching to the fishes, displayed in the study hall of the seminary. The *Brown and White* noted, "Of the original, nothing remains except the arrangement, and even that has received several additions. The faces, which could hardly be called Paduan, might now be considered purely Italian"—a subtle allusion to Chávez's informal nickname in the high-school seminary, after the Italian painter Fra Angelico. Father Bernard Gerbus, a fellow seminarian at the time, describes Chávez's transgressive adaptation of the painting more specifically, noting that, to the alarm of his superiors, Chávez replaced the image of the saint's face with that of the popular Mexican film star Dolores Del Río. Fr. Gerbus also remembers that, while at the novitiate at Mount Airy, Chávez painted an oil portrait of Archbishop McNicholas of Cincinnati directly onto the brick wall of the basement.[10] Including the images of Dolores Del Río and the archbishop in this early artwork set the stage for his experimentation with the faces of townspeople and clergy in the frescoes he painted in New Mexico a few years later.

Chávez continued a more serious experimentation with large-scale frescoes soon after his ordination in 1937. Assigned to Our Lady of Guadalupe Church in Peña Blanca and ministering to nearby churches in Cochiti, Santo Domingo, and San Felipe, he began to experiment in 1938 on the less public spaces of the Peña Blanca mission with large frescoes visually narrating the life of Saint Francis. This art extended the fresco of Saint Francis feeding the birds that

Figure 5.1 Fray Angélico Chávez, Young Francis before Crucifix, *1938, Peña Blanca sacristy (courtesy of the Franciscan Archives, Cincinnati)*

Figure 5.2 Fray Angélico Chávez,
Confirmation of the Rule, *1938,*
Peña Blanca sacristy (courtesy of the
Franciscan Archives, Cincinnati)

Figure 5.3 Fray Angélico Chávez,
Greccio, *1938, Peña Blanca sacristy*
(courtesy of the Franciscan Archives,
Cincinnati)

Chávez had painted earlier in the seminary and served as the proving ground for the Stations of the Cross he would embark on shortly thereafter in the church itself.

On the sacristy walls he painted a progression of images showing the key moments of the narrative of Saint Francis: initially, Francis kneels before the crucifix at San Damiano in his pre-renunciation clothing; the next image, painted across both angled walls of the corner, depicts Francis renouncing his privileged lifestyle, placing his clothing at his father's feet in the presence of the bishop and donning the simple clothing of the peasant (fig. 5.1). Later in the sequence, *Confirmation of the Rule* (fig. 5.2) shows the official recognition of the order, with the supernatural vision of the Virgin and Child in a glowing image in the background. In *Greccio* (fig. 5.3), Saint Francis, as deacon at the midnight mass, prays by the crèche he has built in a cave above Greccio, while the image of the Christ child glows in a halo of light. The visual trope of the glowing depiction of the supernatural again occurs in the mirrorlike aura above Saint Francis as he receives the stigmata (fig. 5.4), a union with Christ so profound that it raises the saint off the ground. The birdlike levitational posture of Francis is echoed in its counterpart above, a fusion of the image of Christ during the Passion with that of the six-winged angel that Francis recounted in his vision. Other subsections of the narrative sequence of paintings in the sacristy depict the investiture of Saint Clare (fig. 5.5); the mission to foreign lands (fig. 5.6); and the death scene, *Transitus* (fig. 5.7).

While the sacristy frescoes illustrate the pivotal moments in the life of Francis, the additional large fresco in the Peña Blanca refectory focuses on the everyday elements of Francis's alternative lifestyle. This triptych portrays Brother Juniper on the left, about to slaughter a pig, Francis and Masseo in the center, and Francis alone in the right panel (fig. 5.8). The triptych echoes, as do the later frescoes of the Via Crucis on the interior church walls of Peña Blanca, the Saint Francis murals in the auditorium of the Museum of Fine Arts in Santa Fe.[11] Of all of the images in the Francis cycle, Chávez was perhaps especially proud of his rendition of the stigmata of Saint Francis (fig. 5.4) and in 1938 designed a Christmas card with a picture of himself painting the image on one side and a verbal greeting on the other, signed "P. Angelico Chavez."

It might be argued that Fray Angélico extended this visual narrative of the life of Saint Francis beyond the sacristy and refectory at Peña Blanca into his restoration work on Our Lady of Guadalupe Church and other neglected churches in the area. Just as Francis undertook the repairs of the church at San Damiano himself after perceiving a voice from the crucifix telling him to do so, Fray Angélico redesigned and rebuilt the facade of the 1869 church in Peña

Figure 5.4 Fray Angélico Chávez,
The Stigmata of St. Francis, *1938,*
Peña Blanca sacristy (courtesy of the
Franciscan Archives, Cincinnati)

Figure 5.5 Fray Angélico Chávez, The
Investiture of St. Clare by St. Francis,
1938, Peña Blanca sacristy (courtesy of
the Franciscan Archives, Cincinnati)

Figure 5.6 Fray Angélico Chávez, Mission to Foreign Lands, *1938, Peña Blanca sacristy (courtesy of the Franciscan Archives, Cincinnati)*

Figure 5.7 Fray Angélico Chávez, Transitus, *1938, Peña Blanca sacristy (courtesy of the Franciscan Archives, Cincinnati)*

Figure 5.8 Fray Angélico Chávez, Brother Juniper, Francis and Masseo, Francis, *1938, Peña Blanca refectory (courtesy of the Franciscan Archives, Cincinnati)*

Blanca, striving to preserve New Mexican history visually and materially; by researching and doing the construction work himself, he hoped to guarantee a historically accurate renovation, in contrast to the hodgepodge of repairs done previously on the church.[12] We get some sense of the physical work involved in a 1941 letter Chávez wrote to Father John Forest McGee, editor of the *Provincial Chronicle*:

> I wonder if from internal evidence, you can deduce my present state! I cannot typewrite, and this pen is held by a rubber-gloved paw! My right hand is badly burned by cement and lime—result of my plastering the front of the church. I'm only half done as the rains, unusual for these parts, are holding me back. As it is, I'll only be able to put on the first coat this fall, which is enough to protect the walls from the weather. Got a new pair of doors for the church front—22 panels and handcarved all. They look nifty.[13]

Besides the interior and exterior remodeling at Peña Blanca and the renovations he undertook at Santa Dorotea Church at Domingo Station, he later remodeled the sanctuary of Saint Joseph Church in Cerrillos. In 1960, during his time at Cerrillos, he restored the Chapel of San Francisco in the dead mining town at Golden, again carefully directing workers and building the tower and front pediment himself, in keeping with the historical model. Replacing the unappealing corrugated tin roof added to the church in 1918 according to a model introduced by French priests (fig. 5.9), Chávez created a stunning new visual presence for the church (fig. 5.10), reasserting an alternate line of history in New Mexico.[14]

Fray Angélico's verbal description of the sanctuary at Peña Blanca, which he remodeled in late summer and early fall of 1938 (fig. 5.11), explains the aesthetic vision he strived to attain in such projects. He notes that he left one gradine so that the altar would not look too low and built a tabernacle dome in reinforced concrete and gold leaf over the original steel safe. He explains the color scheme not visible in the black-and-white photograph he has sent:

> The rear curtains are deep red with horizontal double bars in gold tape. Tapestry is painted on the wall around Father Giles Hukenbeck's "Guadalupe" in Vello, a permanent wall calcimine: ten shades of green with little blazons of cerise and gold. Canopy hangings of velvet pieces, alternately, blue and rose, to match the robes of the Virgin, trimmed with gold fringe and tassels. Larger tassels on corners are from old-time cinctures painted in gold to match.[15]

Working with slim resources, Fray Angélico recycles discarded materials and gives careful attention to both the overall aesthetic appearance of the sacred sanctuary and the close-up, intricate detail of the tabernacle dome, the canopy above, and the "tapestry" he painted on the wall behind the altar.

Along with the architectural renovation, Fray Angélico carried his earlier experimentation with playfully depicting famous people such as Dolores Del Río in religious paintings[16] into a more serious homage that began to encode ordinary people into historical and ecclesiastical remembrance. In 1937–38 he did extensive restoration work at Santa Dorotea Church at Domingo Station (figs. 5.12, 5.13). With a larger aesthetic view, he replaced the front windows on the facade of the chapel with two large frescoes of Saint Jerome and Saint Albert the Great; merging the long view of Church history with a local, close-up view, he painted the faces of two Franciscan priests—his well-loved mentor, Father Jerome Hesse, and the first Franciscan archbishop of Santa Fe, Albert Daeger—into the images of the renowned fathers of the Church. Archbishop Daeger had begun building the chapel when he was a missionary at Domingo, and Fr. Hesse had completed the project. By 1937 the chapel had seriously deteriorated, and with the limited funds and labor of the fifteen families who lived there, Fray Angélico succeeded in restoring the church for a very small sum.[17] Although his efforts at preservation and reconstruction met with set-

Figure 5.9 Chapel of San Francisco, Golden, New Mexico, 1941 (courtesy of the Franciscan Archives, Cincinnati)

Figure 5.10 Chapel of San Francisco, Golden, New Mexico, after renovation by Fray Angélico Chávez, 1961 (courtesy of the Franciscan Archives, Cincinnati)

Figure 5.11 Sanctuary of Our Lady of Guadalupe Church, Peña Blanca, New Mexico, after renovation by Fray Angélico Chávez, 1938 (courtesy of the Franciscan Archives, Cincinnati)

backs (especially the 1987 demolition of the church at Peña Blanca), they constituted a highly visual intervention into the longer narrative of New Mexico history; other priests might have chosen to replace the old structures with more modern buildings.

If architectural renovation and preservation embedded Fray Angélico within the larger macro-narrative of history, his famous frescoes of the Via Crucis at Peña Blanca deployed micro- and macro-narratives together by adding personal, close-up images to the larger story. In a ninety-day period in 1939 he painted eight-by-thirteen-feet murals of the *Stations of the Cross* on the church walls (figs. 5.14, 5.15). In keeping with both aesthetic and liturgical ends, Stations I and XIV were painted across from each other on opposing walls, in the form of an introduction and coda to the main narrative, the points at which the circular procession of the Way of the Cross begins and ends in the liturgical reenactment. Executed as four triptychs and two single panels, the murals depicted the townspeople, Chávez himself, and his sisters as lifesize characters in the visual religious narrative. As he worked, a local woman brought him a photograph of her daughter who had recently died with the request that he

Figure 5.12 Chapel of Santa Dorotea, Domingo Station, New Mexico, built by Father Albert Daeger, O.F.M. (courtesy of the Franciscan Archives, Cincinnati)

Figure 5.13 Chapel of Santa Dorotea, Domingo Station, New Mexico, after renovation and mural painting by Fray Angélico Chávez, 1938 (courtesy of the Franciscan Archives, Cincinnati)

Figure 5.14 Fray Angélico Chávez, Stations of the Cross, *Our Lady of Guadalupe Church, Peña Blanca, New Mexico, 1949 photograph (courtesy of the Franciscan Archives, Cincinnati)*

Figure 5.15 Fray Angélico Chávez, Crucifixion Triptych, *Our Lady of Guadalupe Church, Peña Blanca, New Mexico, 1939 (courtesy of the Franciscan Archives, Cincinnati)*

paint the image into Station VI; the man whose image was used for the centurion in Station IX was later captured on Bataan and died on a Japanese prison ship. In a series of self-reflexive gestures, Fray Angélico inserted himself visually and verbally into the narrative—as Pontius Pilate in Station I (surrounded by pillars and arches modeled on those of Saint Francis Cathedral in Santa Fe, where Fray Angélico had been ordained) and with Latin inscriptions in Stations I and VI, "Angelicus Pinxit."[18]

Chávez painted himself, his family, and the people of Peña Blanca into the visual master narrative displayed on the church walls in much the same way that passion plays, *penitente* processions, *posadas,* and *pastorelas* cast local participants as characters in religious reenactments. The figures of the people in the frescoes thus participate in two semiotic codes with both religious and secular designata. Although today only photos of the murals remain, in the decades when this art survived it visually integrated the micro-narratives of ordinary New Mexicans into the master text of the biblical narrative passed down visually and verbally for centuries.

While the Stations of the Cross visually retell at least one very well-known narrative, the statue of La Conquistadora in Saint Francis Cathedral represents a less widely remembered story. In the late 1940s and early 1950s, Fray Angélico published several narratives on the history of the statue, and, at the strongly visual end of his cultural production, directed a renewal and revival of the statue's visual presence (fig. 5.16). He encouraged local women to make new attire for the statue and had two side altar *retablos* (with paintings originally from the Chapel of Our Lady of Light in Santa Fe, La Castrense) restored and placed together to form a new *reredos* in which the statue would be centrally displayed in the north chapel (fig. 5.17).[19] In addition, in thanksgiving for the end of the war, he had his World War II chaplain's uniform remade into a mantle for La Conquistadora, decorated with his insignia, gold stars, crosses, and the letters "U.S." In the 1950s, he brought gold cloth home from Germany to be made into a dress and cape for the statue; it is lined in red and bears the Chávez family coat of arms. In these ways he visually inscribed himself, his family, and the women who worked with him into the history of both the cathedral and the statue.

Chávez worked with one local woman, Miguelita Hernández, who creatively embedded herself in New Mexican history by sewing many dresses and remaking Archbishop Lamy's cope into a mantle for the statue. Again, under Fray Angélico's direction, micro- and macro-history are combined in the production of visual religious culture. Connie Hernández proudly recounts her family's history when describing her mother Miguelita's role in sewing new garments for the statue, knowing the relation of this work to the larger religious

Figure 5.16 La Conquistadora, *Saint Francis Cathedral, Santa Fe, New Mexico (courtesy of the Franciscan Archives, Cincinnati)*

Figure 5.17 Reredos, *La Conquistadora Chapel, Saint Francis Cathedral, Santa Fe, New Mexico, 1958 (courtesy of the Franciscan Archives, Cincinnati)*

historical narrative. Importantly, this primarily visual vestimentary culture is embedded with narrative. The garments the women sew are like *mandas* or *promesas,* like *milagritos* left on a statue or *retablos* without the accompanying written text. One woman, Mela Ortiz y Pino de Martin, had a dress made for the statue after requesting that her dying mother live one more year. Her sister, Concha Ortiz y Pino de Kleven, gave the Virgin a family necklace, passed on from daughter to daughter since 1780, in petitioning for her brother-in-law Robert Martin's recovery from cancer.[20]

Like the garments, which are primarily visual signifiers with hidden narratives, the statue's pedestal contains a concealed narrative that Fray Angélico reveals only in passing, in the footnote of a scholarly article.[21] Just as he had semiotically embedded himself and local women into the history of the statue and the cathedral, he encouraged his mother and aunts to donate "a more queenly crown" and with his father created a new pedestal to replace one that had been sawed off to fit the statue into a niche. Having asked his father to make the octagonal pine pedestal in a carpentry shop where he worked in Los Alamos, Fray Angélico embellished it himself with bronze paint and Spanish rococo molding from the cathedral museum. Linking his family's role in the creation of this visual signifier to larger historical forces, Fray Angélico argues that the pedestal's provenance from Los Alamos represents "designedly a poetic prayer that La Conquistadora may keep the Satanic horrors of atomic destruction, which originated not far from her throne, firmly suppressed beneath her feet."[22]

Besides his work with La Conquistadora, Fray Angélico used vestimentary semiotics to insert himself both playfully and seriously into history on other occasions. He won the costume contest at the 1926 Fiesta in Santa Fe by appearing as an elegant version of an Argentine gaucho (fig. 5.18). When serving as an army chaplain in Germany in 1952, he designed and had made a set of vestments for himself in the various liturgical colors that reconstructed an original Roman chasuble (fig. 5.19).[23]

If Fray Angélico fictionally became La Conquistadora in the "autobiography" he wrote, he deployed vestimentary signs in a similar way to link his identity to previous historical moments and personages; these dresses, costumes, and vestments insert him visually into a highly public recuperation of religious and secular history.

For the 1986 centennial celebration of Saint Francis Cathedral, Fray Angélico helped to design two important visual monuments—the new church doors and the massive altar screen. He proposed a verbal chronology for sixteen bronze plaques for the church doors that would visually narrate the role of the Church in New Mexico since 1539. Sculptor Donna Quasthoff then designed

Figure 5.18 Fray Angélico Chávez wearing Argentine gaucho costume, Santa Fe, 1926 (courtesy of the Franciscan Archives, Cincinnati)

Figures 5.19 Fray Angélico Chávez in vestments he designed, Kaiserlautern, Germany, 1952 (courtesy of the Franciscan Archives, Cincinnati)

Figure 5.20 Bronze statue of Fray Angélico Chávez and its sculptor, Donna Quasthoff, Santa Fe, 1998

the images and sculpted the panels, paying a small tribute to Fray Angélico in panel 15 by picturing him in the background wearing a beret at the papal coronation of La Conquistadora in 1960.[24] In 1997, Quasthoff paid further homage to Chávez by sculpting the lifesized bronze statue of him that now stands in front of the Fray Angélico Chávez History Library and Photographic Archives in Santa Fe (fig. 5.20), commissioned by Chávez's long-time admirer, Judge Harry Long Bigbee.

Those who stop to visually "read" the serial narrative authored by Fray Angélico and underlying Quasthoff's images on the cathedral door carry on the centuries-old religious pedagogical tradition in which people learn about religion through visual representation. Without accompanying written or oral "captions" to anchor the visual images in this serial narrative, some viewers, especially those not familiar with the history of the region, are unlikely to fully decode the historical specificity of each image; panel 7, for example, is an imagined visual representation of the 1693 ceremony on the plaza of Santa Fe in which General Don Diego de Vargas turned the missions over to the missionaries, and the city to its mayor and council. But whether viewers interpret the images in tandem with the text available in the cathedral brochure or as a more generalized visual narration, the bronze plaques allow one version of history to become visually present, anchoring a selected series of events in a permanent, monumental form.

Fray Angélico made a similar narrative visual contribution to the cathedral by helping to design the 1989 *reredos* depicting saints of the Americas, executed by Robert Lenz, Roberto Lavadie, and Paul Martínez. Each icon in the altar screen contains an implicit narrative about the saint's life, and each participates in the larger historical narrative of Catholicism in the Americas. Fray Angélico's guidance is responsible for the *reredos*' aesthetic harmony because, as Archbishop Sheehan noted at Chávez's funeral (March 22, 1996), when others argued that several New Mexican artists should each paint the icon of one of the saints, Fray Angélico dissented, fearful that the end result would be a hodgepodge.[25]

Chávez's extensive notes and sketches for the design of the *reredos* reveal the harmonious aesthetic effect he envisioned:

This crudely drawn and crudely tinted set of 14 American saints (by a trembling 75-year-old hand) is offered as the basic idea for an altar-screen in St. Francis Cathedral. The subjects are presented more or less *geographically* and *chronologically,* but also with an eye to *color balance.*

The style is envisioned as Byzantine, hence the yellow background of each figure denotes goldleaf to create a general atmosphere of splendor.

The figures themselves both in style and presentation should then be somewhat formally stiff (vaguely suggesting New Mexican *santos,* yet without the latter's too primitive aspect). In other words, with Byzantine majesty.[26]

Chávez's lengthy description of the narratives and visual characteristics of the American saints to be arranged on the *reredos,* along with his substantial contributions in committee meetings about the design of the altar screen, constitute a primarily verbal, sustaining subtext that quietly and implicitly underlies the massive altar screen now displayed in the cathedral.

IMAGETEXTS

Much of Fray Angélico's work lies in the center positions of the visual-verbal continuum. These intermediary, composite texts are sometimes primarily visual with indispensable text, or, alternately, primarily verbal with integral photographs or drawings, sometimes by Fray Angélico himself. They exemplify what Mitchell terms "imagetexts," composite works that I find more useful to view as a rich semiotic hybridity rather than as a competitive battle between the visual and verbal.

The book seal that Fray Angélico designed for the Franciscan house at Peña Blanca in 1938 (fig. 5.21) is a dual yet strongly visual imagetext. The central image of the Virgin of Guadalupe visually invokes both the traditional narrative about the *mestiza* Virgin and simultaneously the name of the mission at which Fray Angélico is stationed. The Franciscan escutcheon and its verbal anchor "Peña Blanca" partially cover the angel that is traditionally beneath the Virgin, and the artist's initials "A. C." diminutively register his presence in the imagetext. The larger letters of the Latin words that surround the image are both subordinate to it yet crucial to the seal's meaning: "From Among the Books of the Friars Minor. At Our Lady of Guadalupe. Peñablanca."[27]

As part of the renovations he did at Our Lady of Guadalupe Church at Peña

Figure 5.21 Fray Angélico Chávez, Book Seal of Peña Blanca, *1938 (*Provincial Chronicle *11 [Spring 1939], p. 126; courtesy of the Franciscan Archives, Cincinnati)*

Figure 5.22 Door of Peña Blanca Church, engraved by Fray Angélico Chávez

Blanca, Fray Angélico asked his uncle Agustín (Gus) Sosaya to make new wooden doors for the church in August 1941. Fray Angélico then carved panels with verbal and visual engravings on the doors, dedicating them to Sosaya's daughter María Dolores, who had died one week before Easter that year of double pneumonia. (fig. 5.22). Alternating vertical and horizontal panels surround a central image of the Sacred Heart on the top half of each door. Two vertical panels facing each other at the center of the two doors depict the emblem of the Franciscan order: a cross rising from the intertwined arms of Christ and Saint Francis. The three other panels on the top half of each door hold inscriptions commemorating the family tragedy and the appearance of the Virgin of Guadalupe in Mexico in 1531. Those on the left door read "En memoria de María Sosaya," "Estas puertas las hizo su Papá" [her father made these doors], "Agosto de 1941." The right door panels are inscribed "Nuestra Señora de Guadalupe," "Es la patrona de este lugar" [Our Lady of Guadalupe is the patroness of this place], "Diciembre de 1531." Fray Angélico links the death of María to the patronal Virgin of Peña Blanca and the Virgin's role in the history of the Americas. Square panels on the bottom halves of the doors give the Spanish names of eleven of the apostles, outlined by appropriate visual images: hearts around Juan, shells around Santiago, arrows around Tomás, fish around Pedro, and crosses around Felipe. In the lower right-hand corner of the right door a panel is left blank, refusing to invoke the name of Judas but making the betraying apostle present precisely by his visual absence. Using the verbal and visual in tandem on these simple wooden church doors, Fray Angélico linked his family history to the long narrative of Christianity in the Old and New Worlds in what he hoped would be a long-lasting tribute to his uncle, his cousin, Franciscanism, and faith.[28]

Fray Angélico created an imagetext for the twenty-fifth anniversary of his ordination in 1962 (fig. 5.23), an illustrated card printed in brown ink, the color of his Franciscan robes. Proud that he was the first native-born Hispano New Mexican to become a Franciscan priest in the nearly four centuries since the Spanish entry into the area, Chávez depicts that history visually with himself as Mass celebrant at the center and the Spanish coat of arms centrally displayed on the front of the altar; to the left, de Vargas holds the statue of La Conquistadora, with other *conquistadores* in the background, while to the right, a Hispano colonial family prays the Mass with him. The painting further invokes de Vargas's Reconquest of Santa Fe in 1692 and 1693 by depicting the Spanish flag to the left and the religious banner with the image of Our Lady of Remedies on the right that the reconquering forces carried with them. Fray Angélico reasserts the importance of the Franciscan presence in New Mexico, depicting this historical scene with the northern New Mexico mountains in the background. These images point to the importance, even on a day celebrating an individual's accomplishments, of the individual's place in the larger community and in history. The large image of the Mass on the card refers not only to Fray Angélico's First Mass in 1937 and his Silver Jubilee Mass in 1962 but to the centuries of Catholic worship since the arrival of the Franciscans. This imagetext also includes a verbal message on the reverse side, in which Fray Angélico invokes the key figures of Saint Francis, La Conquistadora, and Saint Anthony, who were central not only to his life as a priest but to his visual art on several occasions.

Imagetexts were part of his early creative repertoire while he studied for the priesthood. At Duns Scotus College he drew six pages of watercolor cartoons for the *Duns Scotus Athletic Report* from 1931 to 1933 in which he humorously depicted himself and his fellow students visually and verbally. "Water Sports," for example, illustrates Edwin Schick's "superdive," Anthony "Tony" Kroell

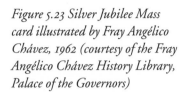

Figure 5.23 Silver Jubilee Mass card illustrated by Fray Angélico Chávez, 1962 (courtesy of the Fray Angélico Chávez History Library, Palace of the Governors)

wearing water wings, and others, including Ignatius Brady (Iggie), Alfred Pimple (Al), and Placid Doyle (Plac) posing as Miss Michigan, Miss Kansas, and Miss Ontario in their swimwear for a beauty contest. In the cartoon "Diamond News" (fig. 5.24), Chávez creates visual puns in the upper left and lower right corners: the "D" of the title is shaped like a baseball diamond, and a shiny diamond gleams inside; in the lower corner, Chávez plays on the sound of the word baseball "plate" by drawing a plate with a steaming meal, knife, and fork.

Although primarily visual, these puns depend on homonymic verbal signifiers with distinctive signifieds to create the intended humor. Chávez depicts himself dizzily on the ground with the caption "Angelico—after he has swung at a high one!" The caption of the lower left panel reads, "Who's the guy with the mask? Nobody Knows. Why the mask: ANSWER: The pen slipped when drawing the face, and so a mask covered the mistake—but it was supposed to be Godfrey Siegwarth!"[29] In various modes Chávez includes his own presence as creator and character in these comic strips both visually and verbally; in addition to the self-referential images in "Diamond News," he signs his name on each page of the cartoon series with a picture rather than letters—a depiction of an angel in various positions. Unlike the popular mass-produced comic strips

Figure 5.24 Fray Angélico Chávez, "Diamond News," Duns Scotus Athletic Report, 1932–33 *(courtesy of the Franciscan Archives, Cincinnati)*

Figure 5.25 Fray Angélico Chávez, "Out of the Centuries," St. Anthony Messenger, *Dec. 1939 (courtesy of* St. Anthony Messenger*)*

and books of the time, Fray Angélico's comics were original watercolor art-works preserved in the athletic scrapbook of the college.

From 1934 to 1940 he published "Out of the Centuries," a monthly column in *St. Anthony Messenger* with little-known facts about the role of Franciscans throughout history. Inspired by Ripley's *Believe It or Not,* these sixty-eight columns draw readers in through Chávez's sketches and neatly lettered captions at the top, with fuller verbal accounts below.[30] Already evidencing a strong interest in historical research, the young Chávez brings obscure infor-mation to a wider Catholic readership in the pleasing format of the imagetext. Readers move back and forth between the visual and verbal elements of the column, enjoying Chávez's humor while learning, for example, that the earliest telescopes were made from a design by Friar Roger Bacon. In one instance, Chávez sketches himself in the column, ministering to Indians as he is ap-proached by members of the Santa Fe Writers' Group (fig. 5.25). The caption reads, "A group of famous writers offered to publish a young missionary's poems—the profits for his missions!"[31] In the text below, Chávez asks readers to buy his new book *Clothed with the Sun* for themselves and their friends, the profits from which will further his missionary work in New Mexico.

Many of Fray Angélico's early publications include his own artwork, which evidences a variety of styles and techniques and establishes a rich relationship with the accompanying text. Dozens of his poems, stories, and articles in *St. Anthony Messenger* feature his drawings, as do *New Mexico Triptych* (1940) and *The Lady from Toledo* (1960). *The Old Faith and Old Glory* (1946), which Chávez wrote for the centenary of the American takeover of New Mexico, includes six hand-drawn and -illustrated maps by Chávez and a cover image invoking the famous photo of the raising of the U.S. flag at Iwo Jima; in Chávez's version, figures representing the native peoples, the Mexican and U.S. armies, and frontiersmen raise the flag while the archbishop looks on; the Cross of the Martyrs stands centrally in the background, as symbolically laden as the U.S. flag (fig. 5.26). Inside the front cover, Chávez anchors the semiosis of this image:

> . . . the figures represent the makers of America in New Mexico. A trapper or scout bases the pole on the ground while soldiers of the Mexican War period do the raising. Native New Mexicans are already lending a hand while an Indian reaches to do his part. Archbishop Lamy stands by imparting courage and guidance. In the center background stands the Cross of the Martyrs as symbol of the Faith planted here by the Spanish Franciscans, and on either side spread the Sangre de Cristo mountains and the Santa Clara Valley cliffs typical of this region.[32]

In addition to cotranslating and elaborately footnoting Fray Francisco Atanasio Domínguez's *The Missions of New Mexico, 1776,* Fray Angélico drew historically accurate sketches of the missions from which another artist made drawings for the book. Chávez made an additional visual contribution to the volume by painting the frontispiece photo of the stone *reredos* installed in the Castrense in Santa Fe around 1760. This retouching of the photo based on extensive historical research, Chávez argued, would give readers an accurate sense of how the *reredos* was likely to have appeared in Domínguez's time.[33]

Much of Fray Angélico's writing relies heavily on visual description and visual intertextuality (of specific *santos,* churches, and sacred places in the fiction, for example), and these images are sometimes explicitly "quoted" or reproduced in the text, as in the case of the Salvador Dalí painting with which Chávez's *The Virgin of Port Lligat* opens.[34] In the 1959 edition of the Port Lligat poem and photograph, Fray Angélico deploys an underlying harmonious con-

THE OLD FAITH AND OLD GLORY
1846 STORY OF THE CHURCH IN NEW MEXICO
SINCE THE AMERICAN OCCUPATION 1946

Figure 5.26 Fray Angélico Chávez, front cover of The Old Faith and Old Glory, *1946 (courtesy of the Archives of the Archdiocese of Santa Fe)*

cept of the visual and verbal, as evidenced in an alternate title he decided upon when he revised the manuscript years later: "A Dalí-Chávez Duet." Although, as I argue elsewhere, Chávez ultimately attempts to attain linguistic closure over both his own verbal text and Dalí's visual one, an important harmonious interaction of the visual and verbal also permeates the work.[35] In "The Setting," the verbal introduction to his poem, for example, he employs the visual metaphor of three images that will structure the poem: the first, his reading of certain images in Dalí's painting, the second, an intellectual metaphor redeveloping the figure of the Sphinx, and the third, which he terms both visual and intellectual, the image from astronomy and nuclear physics of the orderly floating of the constellations and the parallel floating of particles in the interior of the atom. In an ekphrastic gesture, Chávez imagines that the three images are painted on transparent glass or film—the Dalí Madonna, the reconfigured Sphinx, and the cosmic and nuclear galaxies "to reconcile different planes of knowledge and experience in art, science, and theology" (p. xvii).

A closer reading of two of Chávez's many composite texts delineates the noncompetitive partnership of the visual and verbal in his work; both texts also exemplify his continuing identification with images of the Blessed Virgin that have centuries-old roots in New Spain. While Fray Angélico writes himself into some of his tales (the chaplain/driver figure in "The Colonel and the Santo," for example), in his 1954 "autobiography" of La Conquistadora[36] he linguistically becomes the statue, continuing the personifying language that has traditionally been associated with this representation of the Virgin. In a sometimes confusing use of the shifter "I," he merges his own first-person voice with that of the statue. While he can assume the statue's identity verbally in the literary/historical narrative experiment, he cannot do so visually, for the photographs he includes prevent such a merging. Instead, he appears on the cover and in the frontispiece photo touching with admiration and devotion the statue he has helped to re-dress, with her new pedestal, crown, gown, and mantle. The other photos in the book move from the statue's early appearance as a representation of the Assumption to later arrangements of the statue with a rosary or holding the Christ child. As the visual display in the text moves ahead through time, it also moves to different angles, culminating in a final close-up shot. And throughout, Fray Angélico is preoccupied with the statue's appearance—cataloguing and describing its attire at various historical moments and enabling us to see the metamorphoses of La Conquistadora. It is as if he strives to complete his linguistic unification with the statue, begun through the autobiographical "I," by becoming part of its visual semiotic identity—fashioning and writing about the garments, pedestal, and crown. Together, the verbal and visual are tools to achieve this unity, not merely to narrate the statue's story.

In both *New Mexico Triptych* and *From an Altar Screen* (1957), Fray Angélico attempts to merge the verbal genre of the short-story collection with visual religious art forms. Metaphorically, he suggests, these collections are, respectively, a three-paneled New Mexican religious painting and a seven-part *retablo* or *reredos* in which paintings and statues are homologous to the textual settings and characters. Additionally, the stories employ much visual description and intertextual dialogue with the visual artifacts of traditional religious culture in New Mexico. The published volumes use additional visual signifiers to anchor the verbal text, in the form of drawings by either Fr. Chávez or Peter Hurd.[37]

In *New Mexico Triptych*[38] Chávez was able to exercise more authorial visual control by including his own drawings. The book moves to a close-up of the successive panels in the opening *retablo* (fig. 5.27), first by enlarging the relevant illustration (fig. 5.28), then incorporating a motif either from the drawing or related to it into the first illuminated letter of the story, and finally by narratively expanding the visual image in the story. By participating in two semiotic codes, the opening illuminated letter of each story reminds us of the intimate interconnection of the visual and verbal in the book and throughout Fray Angélico's oeuvre. At one instant the initial letter functions as a pictogram connecting the lexème to a counterpart in nature, and at another it returns to its accepted place within the alphabetic script and the verbal text of the story.[39]

The book's third "panel" is the composite narrative "The Hunchback Madonna." The story centers on Mana Seda, an elderly hunchbacked woman who, having been excluded in childhood from May processions in honor of the Blessed Virgin, faithfully gathers flowers each May for other girls to carry in the processions. After a miraculous vision of the Virgin and an encounter with a *santero* who paints an image of the Virgin of Guadalupe on her rebozo and intervenes with the parish priest, Mana Seda is invited to lead the final May procession, and her "tilma" with the Guadalupe painting is displayed above the main altar.

While the small hunchbacked figure at the bottom of the opening illustration (fig. 5.28) is spatially and referentially less important than the large figure of the Virgin floating in the sky above, the deformed curve of Mana Seda's back will become the primary visual motif in the story's closing illustration (fig. 5.29), echoed in the lines of the grave, hillside, and mountains. In the verbal narrative that unfolds between these two drawings, Fray Angélico develops a protofeminist reconfiguration of predominant ideals of female beauty that have even seeped down to popular religious practices. Having internalized the judgmental public view that her identity is coterminous with her deformity, Mana Seda participates in the daily May church processions only as a helper, excluded from the public religious display of ideal femininity. Her encounter

Figure 5.27 Fray Angélico Chávez, frontispiece of New Mexico Triptych, *1940*

Figure 5.28 Fray Angélico Chávez, illustration for "The Hunchback Madonna," New Mexico Triptych, *1940*

Figure 5.29 Fray Angélico Chávez,
closing illustration, "The
Hunchback Madonna," New
Mexico Triptych, *1940*

with the *santero*/Christ figure Esquipula centers on the two characters' visual
and oral retellings of the Virgin of Guadalupe narrative; while Mana Seda's
visual gesture of dropping flowers from her shawl begins the segment of their
narrative exchange of Guadalupe stories, Esquipula's visual marking of her
shawl/ canvas is the culmination of their time together in the adobe hut. The
miracle attributed to the painting of the Virgin in the Mexican Guadalupe
narrative here becomes a protofeminist reversal of the beauty contest; as Mana
Seda's shawl replaces Juan Diego's tilma, her hunchback is painted into the new
Guadalupe image, in much the same way that the contemporary Chicana artist
Yolanda López recasts herself and others as contemporary Guadalupes. Mana
Seda's imperfect back will now become an authorized element of public religious display: she will be invited to walk in the lead position in the last May
procession into the church, the Virgin of Guadalupe painting that incorporates
the lines of her hunchback will be centrally displayed in the *retablo* behind the
altar, and the topography of her grave and shrine will repeat the line of her
back, her flower-filled shawl implicitly covering it, as Fray Angélico's closing
illustration suggests.

Whether working within the strongly verbal, the strongly visual, or composite genres, Fray Angélico Chávez views the two modes of representation as
harmonious rather than embattled, as constantly eliding with each other rather
than behaving as discrete categories. Even in a book such as The *Virgin of Port*

Lligat, in which he strives for interpretive closure over both Dalí's visual text and his own poetic one, an attraction to and affinity with visual representation underlies his poem. In most instances, his desire to narrate is inseparable from his desire to make people see, and vice-versa. One of his earliest poems, "The Painting Poet," focuses on this harmonious connection:

> I plucked a feather with a cactus drill
> From the gray wing of a thrush;
> One side I sharpened to a poet's quill,
> The other end, a painter's brush.
>
> I paint the sage upon the shady ground
> With pigment-words of silver-jades.
> And then I turn my wonder-pen around,
> And with it add the purple shades.[40]

And both of these impulses have succeeded in writing Fray Angélico himself and many ordinary New Mexicans past and present into the master historical narrative that so frequently ignores them.

NOTES

1. Mitchell distinguishes three modes of textual interaction of the visual and the verbal: the image/text, "a problematic gap, cleavage, or rupture in representation"; the image-text, "*relations* of the visual and verbal"; and the imagetext, "composite, synthetic works (or concepts) that combine image and text." See W. J. T. Mitchell, *Picture Theory: Essays on Verbal and Visual Representation* (Chicago: University of Chicago Press, 1994), p. 89 n9.

2. "Here and There," *Brown and White*, 3:8 (May 1927), p.1. Other examples of Chávez's vivid visual writing in this seminary publication include "On the Heights of Eagle Cliff" (Jan. 1927), pp. 1–3, in which he describes a summer day spent hiking in the Mora Valley with a friend, and the poems "May Gems" (May 1926), p. 1, and "The Deserted Mission" (Feb. 1928), p. 5.

3. *The Lady from Toledo* (Fresno, Calif.: Academy Guild Press, 1960).

4. Ibid., p. 7. In all fairness it must be noted that Fray Angélico's "colorful" intuitions and "colorful [narrative] patches" in *The Lady from Toledo* sometimes invoke highly biased racial categories of color as he comes down squarely on the side of the Spanish in narrating the Pueblo Revolt. I refer specifically to his characterization of Diego Naranjo, the "demonic" mulatto believed to have engineered the successful uprising.

5. "New Mexico's Real Romeo and Juliet," *New Mexico Magazine* (Oct. 1976), pp. 12–15, 44–46.

6. Manuel Chávez, "The Angelus," *St. Anthony Messenger* (Nov. 1930), p. 254.

7. "El Santo Closs," *New Mexico Magazine* (Nov.–Dec. 1971), p. 20.

8. In an interview with Father Jack Clark Robinson in 1993, Fray Angélico noted that because of an allergy to milk he nearly died as a baby when his mother tried to give it to him. When a woman came along with a donkey and her foal, he was given donkey's milk. This biographical detail perhaps has some bearing on Fray Angélico's rustic portrait of the mother nursing the young burro, despite Chávez's remembrance that he learned of the story only during his World War II service. Other paintings of scenes of New Mexico include a painting of the old Jemez mission, which he sent to the province in 1938 (*Provincial Chronicle* 11: 2 [Winter 1939], p. 81) and *By East Garcia,* a depiction of the newly built Amelia White estate in the late 1920s, now the School of American Research. In gratitude for the generosity of his aunt, Aurelia Roybal King, who sent him spending money in the seminary, Manuel painted the scene of the beautiful new residence as a gift for her. In July 1999 her daughter, Anna Mae Vigil, donated the painting to the Palace of the Governors in Santa Fe.

9. Interview with Father Godfrey Blank, O.F.M., nephew of Father Floribert Blank, Saint Francis Cathedral friary, Santa Fe, August 6, 1997.

10. "Young Franciscan Paints His Own Church," *St. Anthony Messenger* (May 1940), p. 21; Melvyn Doyle, "In the Month's News," *Brown and White* 5:3 (Dec. 1928), p. 5; interview with Father Bernard Gerbus, Archbishop Leobold Home, Cincinnati, March 22, 1997. Throughout his seminary years Chávez painted scenery for plays and made other artistic contributions, such as the Christmas manger at Duns Scotus College in 1931 and a sketch of Saint Bonaventure completed in February 1932, which was framed and hung in the clerics' recreation room. See "Chronological Journal of Duns Scotus College" (typescript, 1932), pp. 44, 46, on deposit at Franciscan Archives of Saint John the Baptist Province, Cincinnati.

11. While a seminarian in Cincinnati, the young Chávez had written about the museum and its Saint Francis Auditorium, comparing the architecture to the church at Acoma. He used the occasion to tell the history of Fray Juan Ramírez's conversion of the Indians at Acoma in 1644 and the subsequent building of the church on the 357-foot-high precipice. Chávez likened the 1917 museum in Santa Fe to the original "cathedral of the desert" at Acoma. Paying homage to the "lonely friar missionary who labored there 300 years ago," Chávez pointed implicitly to his own future missionary work in New Mexico, and perhaps unsuspectingly to the church frescoes and renovations he would begin to execute soon after his first assignment in Peña Blanca. See Manuel E. Chávez, "The Cathedral of the Desert," *Brown and White* 4: 4 (Jan. 1928), pp. 5–6.

12. Chávez described these previous alterations in a 1943 interview with Harold Butcher: "A gabled farm roof was surmounted with a dog-house belfry and this was capped later on with a mosque-like derby painted with aluminum. False Gothic buttresses were set on the side and at every corner"; see Butcher, "Re-creating a Spanish Mission: Priest, Poet and Painter," *Travel* 80 (March 1943), p. 21.

13. Franciscan Archives of Saint John the Baptist Province, Cincinnati.

14. Ralph Looney, "Mining Camp Church," *New Mexico Magazine* (Oct. 1964), pp. 18–19; and F. Stanley, *The Golden, New Mexico Story* (Pep, Tx.: n.p., 1964), pp. 18–20.

15. "About the Province," *Provincial Chronicle* 11: 2 (Winter 1938 [*sic;* 1939]), p. 84.

16. While studying theology at the Franciscan House of Studies at Oldenburg, Indiana, from 1933 to 1937, Fray Angélico repainted a canvas-covered figure of the risen Christ used

by the seminarians during the Easter liturgy and also in certain pranks in which the figure would be made to "appear" and "disappear." After painting the Christ figure with jet-black hair, a beard, and a staring look, Chávez commented to the other friars that it looked like Haile Selassie, the emperor of Abyssinia, in the news at the time because of Mussolini. The figure then took on the nickname "Haile." See "Resurrectionist Mystery," *Provincial Chronicle* 30 (Summer 1958), pp. 446–47.

17. "Little Gem at Domingo," *Provincial Chronicle* 10 (Apr. 1938), pp. 93–94. The *Chronicle* noted that the two frescoes added "a most pleasing dash of color to the attractive building" and that the people recognized the saints by connecting them to the two friars named after them. Nonetheless, when Father Jerome came to inaugurate the new chapel on Feb. 6, 1938, he "gave the artist missionary in charge a chiding look on seeing the murals and modestly declined to bless the paintings" (p. 94). Archbishop Daeger had died in 1932 after a tragic fall in Santa Fe and thus did not see Fray Angélico's visual tribute to him.

18. Butcher, *op cit.*; Ina Sizer Cassidy, "Fray Angélico Chávez," in "Art and Artists of New Mexico," *New Mexico Magazine* 18 (Mar. 1940), pp. 27, 46; Robert Huber, "Fray Angélico Chávez: 20th Century Renaissance Man," *New Mexico Magazine* 48 (Mar.–Apr. 1970), pp. 18–23; Jim Newton, "Fray Angélico's Artistic Ability Reflected in Church," *Albuquerque Journal*, Aug. 31, 1969, p. C-1; "Young Franciscan Paints His Own Church," *St. Anthony Messenger* (May 1940), p. 21; Ben Gallegos, "Fray Angélico as Muralist," *The New Mexican*, July 9, 1972, pp. 3–4; and Fabián Chávez, "Fray Angélico and the Stations of the Cross," *La Herencia del Norte* (Spring 1998), p. 34–35.

19. Chávez, "Our Lady of the Conquest," in *¡Vivan Las Fiestas!*, ed. Donna Pierce (Santa Fe: Museum of New Mexico, 1985), pp. 18–29; Chávez and Eleanor B. Adams, eds., *The Missions of New Mexico, 1776: A Description by Fray Francisco Atanasio Domínguez* (Albuquerque: University of New Mexico Press, 1956), p.35 n58; and Fray Angélico Chávez, *The Santa Fe Cathedral of St. Francis of Assisi* (Santa Fe: Archdiocese of Santa Fe, 1947), p. 50. Chávez, the author of this booklet on the cathedral, does not give credit to his own central role in renovating the Conquistadora chapel. He complains, however, about subsequent modifications to the esthetic whole he envisioned for the chapel: "Afterwards, unfortunately, the pastor installed stained-glass windows which not only clash with the carefully restored architecture but make the chapel dark and gloomy as well" (ibid.).

20. Emily Drabanski, "Ancient Statue's Attire Made with Devotion," *New Mexico Magazine* (Sept. 1992), pp. 62–66; Camille Flores-Turney, "Dressing La Conquistadora with Care and Devotion," *La Herencia del Norte* (Summer 1994), pp. 31–34; and interview with Connie Hernández, Santa Fe, August 11, 1997. Fray Angélico involved men as well in renewing the devotion to La Conquistadora, such as Pedro Ribera-Ortega, who for many years has served as the *mayordomo* of the confraternity, and the renowned photographer Robert Martin, who documented many historically significant images of the statue and shared some of these photos with others in his handcrafted Christmas cards.

21. I refer to the specific discussion of his family's role in this artistic production, information alluded to only vaguely in the 1954 publication.

22. Chávez, "La Conquistadora Is a Paisana," *El Palacio* 57 (Oct. 1950), p. 306 n16.

23. "The Province and Beyond," *Provincial Chronicle* 24 (Spring 1952), p. 227.

24. Interview with Donna Quasthoff, Santa Fe, August 18, 1998.

25. In a 1987 newspaper article Chávez answers critics who protested the choice of a single artist from outside New Mexico to paint the images. Chávez notes that after discussions with several local painters and much reflection, he realized that no matter how good each separate painting by a different artist for the *reredos* might be, the result would be an unbalanced whole. Robert Lenz, the painter finally selected and a former Franciscan brother, agreed to soften the overtly Byzantine figures he usually painted in order to fit the Romanesque architecture of the cathedral and at the same time invoke the spirit of New Mexico's own primitive church art. See "Selecting Artist for Reredos No Easy Task," *Santa Fe New Mexican*, Dec. 1987.

26. "Reredos," Fray Angélico Chávez Collection, box 520, file 10, Fray Angélico Chávez History Library, Palace of the Governors, Santa Fe.

27. Two years earlier, Fray Angélico had designed his own bookplate with a Latin motto from the New Testament and a drawing of the profile of Fra Angelico da Fiesole, his patron. In the lower left corner he drew a small coat of arms to symbolically represent his name. It portrayed two angel's wings and two keys, pictorially conveying the Spanish word *llaves* (keys), from which the name *Chávez* derived. To the right, his own name appears with the accent marks drawn in. The bookplate was printed in brown ink on white paper to symbolize Franciscanism chromatically. See Angélico Chávez, "How to Make Your Own Bookplate," *Sodalist* 52 (Sept. 1936), pp. 14–15

28. Although the church at Peña Blanca was demolished in 1987, the doors were preserved through the efforts of Manny Sosaya of Albuquerque. Fray Angélico's cousin, Mónica Sosaya, now has them at her home in Santa Fe, a wonderful remembrance of her deceased sister María and her father Agustín Sosaya.

29. See "Water Sports" and "Diamond News," *Duns Scotus Athletic Report*, 1931–32 and 1932–33, Franciscan Archives of Saint John the Baptist Province, Cincinnati. I thank Father Jack Clark Robinson, O.F.M., for sharing this material with me, and Father Dan Anderson for providing color copies of the cartoons.

30. First published in the *New York Globe* in 1918 and today the world's longest-running syndicated newspaper cartoon, "Believe It or Not" by Robert Ripley pictured and recounted bizarre bits of information from around the world. Especially popular in the 1920s and 1930s, the cartoon inspired Fray Angélico to disseminate information on Franciscan history through a parallel humorous, visual/verbal medium.

31. *St. Anthony Messenger* (Dec. 1939), p. 57.

32. Fray Angélico Chávez, *The Old Faith and Old Glory: Story of the Church in New Mexico Since the American Occupation, 1846–1946* (Santa Fe: Archdiocese of Santa Fe, 1946).

33. I include the retouched photo of the Castrense altar screen in the "Imagetexts" section because, as in several of Fray Angélico's works, he writes a lengthy verbal passage to anchor the semiosis of the visual image. In "A Note on the Frontispiece," Chávez explains that he retinted Laura Gilpin's photograph to bring out the faintly visible colors of the altar screen; in addition, he sketched in the walls around the screen according to Domínguez's measurements of the sanctuary and painted the wainscot yellow, following the custom of New Mexico churches. He copied the top border from a Charles Lummis photograph and copied

the image of the painting of Our Lady of Light from the painting in the Loretto Convent in Santa Fe, thought to be the original painting displayed in the *reredos*. Finally, he "restored" the front of the altar according to Domínguez's description, with an oval image of Saint Anthony carved on white stone. See Chávez and Adams, *Missions of New Mexico*, p. xi. Fray Angélico's own drawings of ten of the missions of northern New Mexico accompany his article, "Old Missions in New Mexico," *St. Anthony Messenger* (March 1934), pp. 532–33, 564–65, 574.

34. Fray Angélico Chávez, *The Virgin of Port Lligat* (Fresno, Calif.: Academy Literary Guild, 1959).

35. Ellen McCracken, "A Dalí-Chávez Duet: Visual and Verbal Semiosis in *The Virgin of Port Lligat*," in *Interdigitations: Essays for Irmengard Rauch*, ed. Gerald F. Carr, Wayne Harbert, and Lihua Zhang (New York: Peter Lang, 1999), pp. 681–90. In the new undated typescript, probably prepared in 1989, Chávez notes that he was emboldened to propose the "brazen title pairing off both artist and poet" for a new edition of the book because of the high praise A. Reynolds Morse gave the poem in his 1973 *Poetic Homage to Gala-Salvador Dalí*. See Chávez's foreword for the projected new edition, Fray Angélico Chávez History Library, Palace of the Governors, Santa Fe, p. iv.

36. *La Conquistadora: The Autobiography of an Ancient Statue* (Paterson, N.J.: Saint Anthony Guild Press, 1954).

37. The 1957 edition *From an Altar Screen: El Retablo: Tales From New Mexico* (New York: Farrar, Straus and Cudahy) transposes two of Hurd's illustrations in the last two stories. The 1977 edition (Santa Fe: William Gannon) correctly places the illustrations and retitles the volume *When the Santos Talked: A Retablo of New Mexico Tales*. Chávez notes that New York publishers incorrectly titled the book *From an Altar Screen* in the earlier edition. See "Southwestern Bookshelf," *New Mexico Magazine* (June 1977), p. 31.

38. Fray Angélico Chávez, *New Mexico Triptych* (Paterson, N.J.: Saint Anthony Guild Press, 1940).

39. In emphasizing the strong linkage of the verbal and the visual in Fray Angélico's work, I do not wish to gloss over important differences in the two semiotic systems. The successive reading moments of the illuminated letter reveal that the religious icon visible at the pictographic level functions through similitude, while the lexème in the alphabetic code functions through difference.

40. Fray Angélico Chávez, "Cantares: Canticles and Poems of Youth, 1925–1932," type-written bound book prepared by Fray Angélico Chávez and given to his parents on the occasion of his profession of solemn vows, August 16, 1933, Fray Angélico Chávez History Library, Palace of the Governors, Santa Fe, p. 12.

CHAPTER SIX

PAINTING THE WORD / WORDING THE PAINTING:

Allegory and Intertextuality in *The Virgin of Port Lligat* by Fray Angélico Chávez[1]

MANUEL M. MARTÍN-RODRÍGUEZ
Texas A & M University

In recent decades, a resurgent interest in the relationship between poetry and painting has revived the traditional debates on the (non)mimetic nature of art, as well as on the relationship between "natural signs" (of iconic nature) and "arbitrary signs" (of symbolic nature). Not surprisingly, this revival has been accompanied by a revision of linguistic and semiotic approaches to the nature of the sign, which has taken a central role in the area of literary and artistic criticism. As summarized by Wendy Steiner, "At the beginning of this century, the *ut pictura poesis* controversy stood as a mere historical curiosity. . . . But if we turn half a century later to the conference programs of institutions of literary studies . . . we find the comparison of painting to literature a major topic of concern. A revolution in critical thinking has taken place, a revolution that seems clearly related to the spread of structuralism and semiotics . . . and the correspondent interest among recent philosophers in linguistics and aesthetic issues."[2]

This renewed preoccupation with the overall relationship between the plastic and the literary arts has generated considerable attention to Horace's classical dictum *ut pictura poesis,* as well as to the notion of ekphrasis. The ekphrastic literary work uses words to create a plastic object for the mind's eye.[3] As Krieger further explores in his book, the major tension arising in this verbal recreation of an object from the plastic arts results from the predominantly spatial structure of the latter, whereas the former, literature, is marked by the implicit temporality of language.[4]

In the context of these recent developments in linguistics, semiotics, literary and art theory, Fray Angélico Chávez's *The Virgin of Port Lligat* stands out as an interesting ekphrastic endeavor.[5] In the 113-line poem, Chávez is largely inspired by Salvador Dalí's painting *The Madonna of Port Lligat* (1951), which is reproduced on the dust jacket and frontispiece of the book edition.[6] Dalí presents Madonna and Child as floating slightly above her throne, a throne whose bottom part resembles a mixture of altarpiece and pedestal. Parts of the throne are also suspended in midair, as is the background landscape of Port Lligat. Directly above the Madonna, an egg dangles from a floating seashell, attached to it by a string. Most strikingly, the Madonna's bosom is represented as a square cut, which serves as a frame for the Child's figure. A similar square cut is found in the Child's breast, markedly resembling an altar's tabernacle, particularly since this square contains a floating piece of bread reminiscent of the consecrated hosts kept in such tabernacles. Several other motifs complete the painting: a fish, a bread basket, a couple of smaller human figures in the background, a rhinoceros, flowers, and a few others.

As central as this painting is for Chávez's poem, it should be noted that Fray Angélico also draws his inspiration from classical mythology, as well as from nuclear physics and astronomy. The resulting richness of Chávez's imagery and the interconnection of the different referential and cultural fields from which this imagery is drawn are remarkable. At the same time Chávez's poetic ambition results in an opening up of his text to alternative readings that undermine his unifying allegorical attempt.

Given its multiple sources of inspiration, Fray Angélico's poem moves beyond mere description of the painting, to an ambitious and artistically successful blending of religion, science, painting, and poetry. In that sense, the poem is broader in scope than a simple ekphrasis, turning Dali's painting into an enigmatic emblem in need of interpretation, much in the tradition explored by Krieger: "As visual companion to the poem, the emblem, which is no longer anything like a mimetic representation, seems cryptic and in need of explication, so that it leans upon a text whose verbal completeness now permits *it* to claim primacy."[7]

Indeed, Dali's *The Madonna of Port Lligat* is a surrealistic painting of ambiguous religious symbolism that requires a great deal of interpretation. A Franciscan priest, Fray Angélico is in a privileged position to turn the somewhat vague or enigmatic religious references in Dali's painting into a detailed and carefully constructed *alegoría a lo divino*[8] that places every iconic and linguistic image, in both painting and poem, at the service of a central metaphor: Christ the Child as both riddle and answer of the enigmatic text. In doing so, Fray Angélico taps on well-established literary precedents, from the English metaphysical poets to Sor Juana Inés de la Cruz (as Paul Horgan has observed)[9], as well as many

Spanish Baroque poets, including Lope de Vega, Calderón, and Góngora. Similarly to these poets, who often utilized the *glosa* (gloss) to transform a lay stanza into a religious allegory, Fray Angélico's use of the Dalí painting (as well as motifs from mythology, physics, and astronomy) allows him to construct a complex allegory of the Holy Trinity and of the life of Christ, from His birth to His death and resurrection. In the process, Chávez manages to reverse the relationship between painting and poem, having the latter take priority over the former.

The idea of an enigma to be solved is a thematic and imagistic focus in Chávez's poem, especially in the important intertextual presence of the mythical Sphinx of Thebes from Sophoclean drama. With the addition of this image (not explicitly present in Dalí's painting), Chávez hinges his poem on a triptych of images that serves as the primary device at the referential and allegorical levels: the Sphinx, the atom, and the Madonna.[10] Emphasizing the centrality of this triad, Fray Angélico explains it in a prologue to the poem, entitled "The Setting." In it, the poet discusses the Madonna pictorial genre in the Renaissance tradition and Dalí's appropriation and subversion of that tradition, the relevance of the mythological Sphinx and Chávez's own rephrasing of it, and what he terms a double image: the description of the atom in nuclear physics combined with the astronomical description of floating constellations. This third element is also closely related to Dalí's painting, since Dalí describes his work as representing spirituality and the atomic system, much in line with his other "atomic" paintings of the time.[11]

The choice of this ternary imagistic structure for *The Virgin* is in perfect synchrony with the religious tradition to which Fray Angélico Chávez adheres. It may even be motivated by his dedication of the book to a fellow Franciscan, John Duns Scotus, the Doctor Subtilis of the Middle Ages, one of whose primary concerns was precisely the impossibility of rationally comprehending that God is three persons.[12] With a subtle ability worthy of Scotus himself, Chávez manages to incorporate the notion of the Holy Trinity into a complex cultural, scientific, and visual frame of reference that amounts to a poetically convincing rendering of the mystery, an approach we could term his "atomic argument," in allusion to what is usually known in philosophy as the ontological argument—that is, Saint Anselm's proof for the existence of God. Yet, inasmuch as he draws upon Sophoclean tragedy and surrealistic painting, Chávez's attempt results in the opening up of certain problematic lines of reading. Although mainly suppressed by the poem and the accompanying explanation of it, these lines of reading remain part of a visible subtext that erodes from within his carefully constructed allegory.

His approaching the mystery of the Holy Trinity is done in an almost tangential way at first, since the poem begins with a reference to the Sphinx in the initial description of the Virgin Mary:

> The Sphinx of this our age is gentle-formed and sweet
> Not only in her woman's face and breast, for she
> Is all Eve's daughter to her feet.
> Whatever there may be of lioness
> Is energy;
> Whatever wings, a hovering loveliness
> Heedless of need for leaning hard on pedestal of stone,
> Untouched and touching nothing, free (pp. 1–3).[13]

Only closer to the end, in lines 76–81, is the mystery confronted directly, with a rhetorical question that explains it in a religious and scientific context, by way of an analogy to the atom's structure:

> And days before, when earth and heaven were begun
> With but a Word on which the Spirit swept in flight,
> He spoke and breathed as *Elohim*;
> Might not the tiniest indivisibles demand
> That even the infinitely opposite Extreme
> Have Proton, mutual Pneum, and still be One? (pp. 23–25)

But this apparent delay should not be confusing, since the poem has carefully prepared us to understand that every one of its images and concepts are like stars of a same constellation (if I may appropriate Chávez's own imagery); that is, that they are at the service of a central riddle that we should be able to recognize and solve. As such, all images are interconnected and mutually necessary for interpretability. Thus, the complexity of the book and the mastery with which Chávez relates his three main images with the others in the poem result in a constant protention-retention movement for the reader, since understanding of any given image depends on the reader's ability to place it within the context of previous ones, while imagining new developments in subsequent lines.

From what I have termed his atomic argument of representing visually and conceptually the mystery of the Holy Trinity, Chávez extends his poetic powers to explain Christ's miraculous conception. In order to do so, he invokes the galaxies in clearly a Franciscan and, once again, ternary way (the sun, the moon, and the Star of Bethlehem):

> Praised be the Lord for Brother Sun
> And Sister Moon, for all great things above . . .
> But most of all for that one Sister Star
> That pointed to a stall
> Where ox and ass one night
> Saw in a wailing Nova how the Word that fashioned all,
> By fusing with a maiden's molecules, geared infinite
> To nuclear. (pp. 25–27)

The mystery of Christ's conception is understood above as a process of the nuclear fusion of "a maiden's molecules" and God as "the Word that fashioned all." "Nuclear" refers both to atomic energy (in particular to the atom as visual symbol of the Holy Trinity) and to the nucleus or center of the egg.[14] The fertilized ovum of the Virgin Mary, from the previous quotation, is thus related to the egg that in the painting is suspended over the Madonna and Child, an image previously explained by Chávez in his notes as "a common symbol of Life and Resurrection" (pp. 49–51).

With this reference, then, the poem brings us back to the beginning of the text (or even further back, to the painting as pre-text), rendering understandable what in Dalí is somewhat enigmatic: the suspended egg, according to Chávez, emblematically contains the Holy Trinity, since it is an image of the fertilizing Word (God the father), the unborn baby (God the son), and the power of the Holy Spirit to "fus[e] with a maiden's molecules" (God the Holy Spirit, also implicit in the word "pneum" in line 81).[15] But at the same time, in the visual context of the painting, the egg is made to stand for the more traditional image of the eye within a triangle, which usually represents God the father, thus forming another triad with the Madonna and Child.

In this reference to the poem's beginning, Chávez clarifies how the "riddle" of the Holy Trinity is combined poetically and thematically with Sophocles's riddle and with Dalí's enigmatic presentation of his subject. The first line of the poem, perhaps the most beautifully crafted in the book, compared the Virgin Mary with the Sophoclean Sphinx, preparing us to be on the alert for the Virgin's own riddle. Fray Angélico's prologue had previously recalled the riddle of the mythic Sphinx of Thebes, as well as the consequences associated with the passersby's failure to solve it. By contrast, this modern, sweet Sphinx's riddle turns out to be her son, whom she displays on her lap for everyone to admire. According to the poem, Jesus Christ, as a human being, epitomizes the three phases of humanity in Sophocles's riddle, despite his early death by crucifixion. The image of the cane is thus substituted with the cross in Chávez's reworking of the riddle in the epiphanic lines 104–6, which are reserved a page of their own:

Oh, blessed little pattering in Bethlehem!
Oh, sacred walking to and from Jerusalem!
Oh, dragging cross to Calvary! (p. 33)

The Sphinx in this new riddle is also freed from her cruel job of devouring passersby, since Christ's own sacrifice, according to Christian doctrine, redeems humanity. Consequently, the poem ends on a happy note of resurrection (the only important aspect of Christ's story absent from the riddle) and a recalling of the miracle of the multiplication of loaves and fishes (also suggested in the painting by several elements, including the piece of bread at the Child's breast, the fish, a couple of bread baskets, and an ear of wheat):

The central Infant watches how His playing brings
More births in bread through lovelier alchemy
To fill the hungry with good things. (p. 35)

The poem's ability to develop its topic in bold images and to relate them in an aesthetically convincing form should be commended. And yet, Chávez's impressive effort to conjoin all his intertextual and visual references into an integrated system of religious allegory, while poetically effective, is somewhat unstable. The intertextual use of Sophoclean tragedy complicates Fray Angélico's ternary allegorical system by introducing a darker triad, the Oedipal triangle. While Chávez in his prologue explains the fate of the passersby who failed to solve the Sphinx's riddle, he carefully sidesteps the story of Sophocles's protagonist, the one who in effect did solve the riddle. But Oedipus's solving of the Sphinx's enigma precipitates tragedy by having him wed his own mother, after having killed his father. The implications of this subtext for the religious story that Chávez celebrates are devastating, as they are for its relation to Dalí's painting—even if the painting is not explicitly connected to the Sophoclean intertext. Indeed, the myth plays an important role in earlier paintings by Dalí. As Whitney Chadwick notes, "According to Dalí, in an inversion of Freud's thesis, the father sees the son as a rival for the mother's affections and slays him. Freud had concentrated his analysis on the incestuous marriage between Oedipus and his mother; Dalí focuses on Laius's decision to kill the infant in order to prevent the fulfilling of a prophecy in which the child will slay the father."[16] In that light, it could be argued that the Oedipal intertext is also part of *The Madonna,* and that it is most visible in the symbolic erasing of the father figure (substituted in the painting by an egg). Oedipus's final blinding of himself in remorse could also find a pictorial correspondent in the fact that both the Madonna and the Child appear with closed eyes; further, the two square cuts in the bodies of the Madonna and the Child are somewhat reminiscent of hollow orbits.[17]

Similarly worthy of problematizing is Fray Angélico's decision not to interpret certain elements of Dalí's painting that reinforce the sexual connotations present in the Sophoclean intertext. Thus, in a note contained in his prologue, Chávez inserts the following disclaimer: "The poet purposely ignored the artist's strictly private symbols, such as the rhinoceros in the pedestal, the shell metamorphoses in the background, and other minute details" (p. xv). It is problematic indeed for Chávez to claim that certain symbols in the painting are "strictly private," while others he chooses to interpret (the egg, the square cuts, etc.) are not. Moreover, since metamorphosis could be said to be at the heart of the surrealist approach to classical myths,[18] it seems difficult to avoid an interpretation of those images that Chávez discards. Fray Angélico's refusal to explicate what he calls "private" symbols is in line with his sidestepping of the Oedipal story, since the rhinoceros and the shells are charged with sexual undertones as well. In the case of the rhinoceros, an image sexually charged because of the phallic tusks, which are believed to possess aphrodisiac power, Fray Angélico's withdrawal is perhaps understandable.[19] That is not the case, at least not immediately, with the shells, an image frequently associated with birth, women, and fertility, associations which would have easily reinforced Chávez's own imagery.[20]

A possible key for Chávez's refusal to engage in an analysis of this imagery can be found in an earlier painting by Dalí, *Leda atómica* (1949), which had already elaborated much of what is to be found in *The Madonna of Port Lligat*. As in the latter painting, the earlier work uses Gala (Dalí's wife) as a model. But where the Madonna appears fully clothed, Leda appeared naked, floating over a broken eggshell and a throne, next to a swan; a book and two egg-shaped objects are also floating in the foreground. The two paintings reflect a common interest in the atomic (the floating subject), as well as in the union of gods with a woman. To be certain, though, *The Madonna* was painted during Dalí's controversial phase in which he claimed to have embraced the Catholic faith, and a preliminary, simpler version of the painting was even shown to Pope Pius XII during a private audience.[21] Therefore, the religious force of the poem is more intense than the purely mythical one of *Leda*, and it is appropriate that the floating Madonna could be interpreted by Chávez as "Untouched and touching nothing" (p. 3), in a clear reference to the virgin birth, whereas in Leda's case sexual intercourse is said to have been consummated,[22] since in Greek mythology Leda was made pregnant by Zeus, who took the shape of a swan to deceive her (metamorphosis once again entering into play). Afterwards, Leda gave birth to two eggs: Castor and Pollux were born out of one, Clytemnestra and Helen out of the other.[23] The new symbolism gained by the shells and the egg in examining this painting clearly destabilizes Fray Angélico's interpretation of *The Madonna*, while a further connection between the story of Leda and Chávez's poem—via astrology—emerges in the fact that Castor and Pollux, after their deaths, were supposedly transformed in the stars known as the Gemini constellation. Clytemnestra, on the other hand, is the subject of a story of adultery and murder (she kills her husband Agamemnon to avoid his discovery of her adulterous life) and is finally slain by her own son, Orestes, aided by his sister Electra. These incidents are recreated in Aeschylus's *Orestes,* as well as in Sophocles's *Electra.* Interestingly, then, *Leda atómica* brings us back to Sophocles, sex, and parricide.

Whether or not Fray Angélico had seen this earlier painting by Dalí, it is clear that he was familiar with Greek mythology and must have seen the connections that his poem could open up for his readership. His choice of intertextual references (both visual and literary) constantly subvert the allegorical religious impulse of his poem with images that point to sex, seduction, adultery, rape, parricide, and matricide.

The poetic closure sought by Chávez's masterful attempt at allegory in *The Virgin of Port Lligat* is ultimately subverted by intertextual openness, and the ternary structures that he devises as organizing forces for his glorification of the Holy Trinity are shattered by the mythological triangles they recall for the reader.[24] Consequently, although Fray Angélico clearly intends his poem to subordinate painting, mythology, and science to religious beliefs and dogma, a careful contextualization of *The Virgin* seems to demonstrate the impossibility of such an endeavor, since artistic signs resist monological significance in the way they engage in a dialogue with other signs and texts.

NOTES

1. I would like to thank John Eipper and Michael Giordano for their insightful comments on this essay.

2. Wendy Steiner, *The Colors of Rhetoric: Problems in the Relation between Modern Literature and Painting* (Chicago: University of Chicago Press, 1982), p. 19.

3. Murray Krieger, *Ekphrasis: The Illusion of the Natural Sign* (Baltimore: Johns Hopkins University Press, 1992), p. 16.

4. On this issue see Krieger, *Ekphrasis,* chapter 7. Recent developments in semiotic and art theory have complicated the question by pointing towards a more temporal reading of paintings, as well as to the need to interpret visual signs as discrete, a phenomenon that Krieger acknowledges on pp. 206–7.

5. Fray Angélico Chávez, *The Virgin of Port Lligat* (Fresno, Calif.: Academy Library

Guild, 1959). The poem first appeared in *Spirit: A Magazine of Poetry* 23 (May 1956), pp. 49–51. All quotations are from the 1959 book.

6. There are two versions of the painting, a simpler one from 1949 and the more elaborate version from 1951, which is the one that inspires Chávez. For a contextualization of these paintings within Dalí's religious period, see Meredith Etherington-Smith, *The Persistence of Memory: A Biography of Dalí* (New York: Random House, 1992), pp. 327ff.

7. Krieger, *Ekphrasis,* p. 19; emphasis in the original.

8. I am purposefully leaving the term *alegoría a lo divino* in Spanish, since it is my intention to link Chávez with the Baroque Spanish poets who similarly used this type of religious allegory. On the other hand, Chávez's poem may be also read as a forerunner of more recent attempts by Hispanic poets to blend religion and science, such as those of Ernesto Cardenal in *Cántico cósmico* (Managua: Nueva Nicaragua, 1989). In this light, an interesting precedent is found in Sor Juana Inés de la Cruz's long poem "Sueño," an ambitious attempt to blend science and poetry.

9. Horgan's ideas are quoted on the jacket copy of *The Virgin*'s first edition. Chávez himself commented on his fascination with Blake's poetry in his *Selected Poems, With an Apologia* (Santa Fe: Press of the Territorian, 1969).

10. Although the Sphinx is not a visible part of Dalí's *The Madonna,* it was one of the cherished myths of surrealist painting. Dalí had made it the subject of several earlier works, such as *Remorse or Sunken Sphinx* (1931) and *Shirley Temple, The Youngest Monster Sacred to the Cinema of her Time* (1939), which depicts the Sphinx with the face of the child actress. For an analysis of myths in surrealist painting, see Whitney Chadwick, *Myth in Surrealist Painting, 1929–1939* (Ann Arbor: UMI Research Press, 1980).

11. Etherington-Smith, *The Persistence of Memory,* pp. 330–31. Nuclear energy is also interesting on a different level for a New Mexican like Chávez: as he points out in one of his notes to the poem, "by a most uncanny coincidence . . . , the secret project of the first atomic test, and the site of the first nuclear explosion in New Mexico, were called 'Trinity.'"

12. For Duns Scotus's ideas on metaphysics and natural theology see Frederick Copleston, S.J., *Medieval Philosophy* vol. 2 of *A History of Philosophy* (1962; New York: Doubleday, 1993), particularly chapter XLVIII.

13. The text of the poem is printed on the odd pages only in the book edition. The even pages contain a drawing representing an atom. Original emphasis and capitalization are preserved.

14. Clearly, the image also has other biological ramifications beyond those connected to reproduction, since most animal cells have an egg-shaped or spherical central mass of protoplasm, which is necessary for growth as well as reproduction.

15. In his notes, Chávez comments on "pneum," to defend his using the term in the context of atomic science: "*Pneum,* not a nuclear scientific term like *proton,* but similar in Greek derivation, means 'spirit'" (p. 59).

16. Chadwick, *Myth and Surrealist Painting,* p. 23. Chadwick also explores how this relates to Dalí's own problems with his father, as well as to his resulting pictorial interest in the William Tell story.

17. Somewhat similar squares—this time representing framed paintings—had been used

by Dalí to depict the eyes of the actress in his famous *Face of Mae West which May Be Used as an Apartment* (c. 1935).

18. Chadwick, *Myth and Surrealist Painting*, p. 14.

19. On the other hand, it should be kept in mind how the rhinoceros combines with Greek art in Dalí's *Rhinocerontic Disintegration of Illisus of Phidias* (1954), in which metamorphosis also plays a central role. In the painting, we see the transformation of the naked human figure (which sports a hollowed chest with a cube inside) into a rhinoceros, with the animal's tusks replacing the phallus.

20. On the symbolism of shells, see Juan Eduardo Cirlot, *Diccionario de símbolos* (Barcelona: Labor, 1988), p. 143. In the context of painting, a cherished subject of representation that entails such use of the shell is the birth of Venus. In Dalí's painting *Rhinocerontic Gooseflesh* (1956), the rhinoceros and the shell combine in what appears to be a version of the birth of Venus myth, as a female naked body (missing one arm, both feet, and the head) floats over a shell and the ocean. To be certain, there are other images in Dalí's *The Madonna* that could be charged with sexual symbolism, such as the egg, but I will be concentrating on those that Chávez opts not to discuss.

21. Meryle Secrest, *Salvador Dalí* (New York: E. P. Dutton, 1987), p. 192.

22. Bordering on bestiality, one might add, and hence perhaps Fray Angélico's uneasiness with the rhinoceros.

23. The myth has several versions and is narrated in many works of reference. I have followed the description in Constantino Falcón Martínez, Emilio Fernández-Galiano, and Raquel López Melero. *Diccionario de la mitología clásica*, 2 vols. (Madrid: Alianza, 1980), pp. 383–84.

24. Interestingly, in her psychoanalytic analysis of the Oedipal myth as the story of a quest for knowledge, Laura Mulvey arrives at a similar conclusion when she states, "Curiosity and the riddling spirit of the Sphinx activate questions that open up the closure of repression and maintain the force of an 'uncertainty principle'"; see Laura Mulvey, *Visual and Other Pleasures* (Bloomington: Indiana University Press, 1989), p. 200. Here, it is almost as if Chávez's own intellectual curiosity unleashed the unconscious stories that his allegory attempts to repress. After all, as Barbara Johnson has suggested, "intertextuality designates the multitude of ways a text has of not being self-contained, of being traversed by otherness"; see Barbara Johnson, *A World of Difference* (Baltimore: Johns Hopkins University Press, 1987), p. 116.

CHAPTER SEVEN

RECOVERING THE NOBLE
SPANISH SOUL

CLARK COLAHAN
Whitman College, Walla Walla

Spain, and Spanish culture as Fray Angélico understood it, appear frequently in his writings. Both the country and its customs often generate details in his New Mexican settings, but the passing references are elusive, sometimes seemingly contradictory. Yet Chávez's fascination with Spain was the starting point for much that he wrote.

Genaro Padilla notes accurately that his stories "typically pit representatives of the upper class . . . against families of mixed blood."[1] But surprisingly, throughout his writings it becomes clear that Chávez considered the majority of Hispanic New Mexicans, regardless of their ancestry, as aristocrats in a moral sense, representing the noble elements within what he called the "Spanish soul."

His work as a whole does not attack the idea of aristocracy. On the contrary, it reinterprets the concept, affirming, as we shall see when examining his *My Penitente Land,* that everyone who has inherited authentic Spanish culture is heir to a noble legacy, regardless of social station. If in his stories he preferred mixed-blood New Mexicans over haughty claimants to a noble family tree, it is because he judged the humility of the mestizo more truly noble than the pride of those who boast of their lineage.

In "A Romeo and Juliet Story in Early New Mexico" we have an unmistakable example of the antithesis Chávez established between some Spanish aristocrats, arrogant and stand-offish, and the best elements of the national character, often found among commoners: "In the end, it all had turned out into a pitched battle between the Spanish-born Bustamantes of the mountains of Santander and a lone youth from the hills of Santa Fe with more Indian than

Spanish blood in his lovelorn heart. And Spain had won, apparently, forgetting for the nonce that all her songs and tales give true love the victory in the end."[2] Still, paradoxically, Chávez wrote a voluminous study of New Mexican genealogies, *Origins of New Mexico Families,* tracing as many New Mexicans as possible back to Spain and the Spanish aristocracy.

On balance, then, do his stories tell us that mestizo peasants have always been the moral leaders of New Mexican society, corrupt aristocrats with vaunted ties to Spain the true villains? Such is the impression he sometimes gives, and the idea would harmonize well with Franciscan ideals of humility and poverty. But no, not always, since for Chávez respect for colonial leaders (who included his own ancestors) and affection for their twentieth-century descendants led him to accept the Hispanic version of Saint Francis, one with less extreme attitudes toward social equality.

Padilla points in the short stories to the writer's vision of a colonial period improved by "imaginary resolution of intracultural conflict."[3] But Chávez's lack of ideological consistency, his use of the imaginary in this matter, was not capricious, or primarily religious. In the simplest terms, Chávez brought together in his vision, as well as he could, the best elements in his cultural heritage, though it was as uneven as any other.

If his artistic amalgam was not without its paradoxes, it met his existential needs and has met those of uncounted other New Mexicans who have thought of themselves as Spanish. Chávez would probably have said that the same was true throughout the colonial history of Spanish New Mexico, where idealism and opportunism coexisted in prominent conflict without the practitioners seriously questioning the basic value of the combination. Similarly, he was not willing to relinquish an inherited and self-affirming view of his identity as a Spanish New Mexican. For Chávez, born in the aftermath of the U.S. conquest, cultural self-doubt was a road that would have led him dangerously close to abandoning his self-esteem along with his heritage.

Some Chicano critics have failed to recognize that the embrace of Spanish culture by Chávez responds to the same needs that led early-twentieth-century Mexican writers to embrace Aztec culture as their nation's real identity. One was a reaction against the recent U.S. invasion and takeover of New Mexico, the other against an older Spanish imperialism. A defeated Spain was the Camelot to which the oppressed looked nostalgically in New Mexico, although it was still seen as the hated overlord south of El Paso.[4]

If the stories introduce some ambiguity about Chávez's attitude toward Spanish social structure, they make very clear that Chávez's strongest attraction to Spain was in the area of spirituality, its religious tradition. Importantly, he chose for himself the title "Fray," used by early missionaries, and emulated their work in New Mexican villages. In some of his narratives, references to Spanish religion connote an individual's moral purity. In "The Hunchback Madonna" Esquipula places on Mana Seda "a precious veil of Spanish lace"[5] as a way of marking her spiritual worth and beauty.

In other stories, the allusions are more to community values. In "The Angel's New Wings," Nabor, the *santero,* recalls times gone by when he was a boy: "those days breathed reverence and faith . . . his father leading the singing of old Spanish carols."[6] The Spanish carols represent the sustaining beliefs and customs passed down from parent to child and shared by neighbors. They are the outward manifestation of the inner peace that once graced most of the members of the community.

The value of traditional religion for the community is even more pronounced in "The Penitente Thief," in which Chávez describes "a large chalice which had come with the first settlers and which was used only on big feasts. It was solid gold, not merely gold-plated . . . San Ramón's chief treasure."[7] The focus on solid gold suggests the cultural authenticity and great worth of Spanish Catholicism for Spanish New Mexicans. That the object is a communion cup, and one used only on feast days, points toward the shared bond of the Last Supper and communal celebrations. The traditional nature of that bond is revealed by the assertion that the chalice had come with the first settlers.

Chávez's *My Penitente Land* discloses the extent of his conscious self-identification with Spanish heritage. The opening line of the first chapter, which describes the crossing of the Rio Grande at El Paso by Oñate's band of settlers in 1598, is told in the first person, as if it were Chávez's own birth. The autobiographical material in the book also confirms that at the root of his commitment to Spanish identity was hurt pride early in life. As an adult writer he recalled becoming aware, when young, of the "subconscious feeling of racial superiority" on the part of the French priests who replaced the native New Mexican clergy."[8] Chávez points to another formative childhood experience: his mother's frustration at being conscious of her "Spanish individuality" but unable to explain it.[9] There is little doubt that he was powerfully moved by a desire to vindicate his worth as a Spanish New Mexican, and that such vindication required the clarity and dignity of an ethnic self-knowledge he found painfully lacking in his own family.

What that dignified self-identity might be suggested itself to him early in life in the conviction that Castilian Catholicism, not the officially preferred Anglo or French or German Christianity of his childhood, was closer to Jesus' religion and way of seeing the world. He felt, for example, that the Crucifixion could not have been so trivially pretty or taken place in such an attractive green landscape as portrayed in the Catholic "holy cards" produced in New York. He perceived "by some unerring instinct" an inauthenticity in the non-Spanish religious authorities to which he was subject, and he was quick to confirm it by the thought that most of sacred history had taken place elsewhere, "in a land very much like mine."[10] Of course, it is not hard to think of ways in which biblical Palestine and colonial New Mexico were different, but as Chávez himself often pointed out, his work is art, not science.

As part of recasting New Mexican life as biblical, Chávez found a tendency to asceticism in New Mexican life, reflected in the penitential brotherhoods. He pointed to what he believed to be parallels in the earliest Hebrew society, companies of "quasi penitential" Nazarites, who abstained from drinking wine and cutting their hair. For Chávez, Jesus himself was not only a Nazarene but such a Nazarite, an expression of an ascetic mindset also characteristic of Spanish New Mexico.[11]

To link biblical times with seventeenth-century Spain and New Mexico, Chávez turned next to the Franciscans. He viewed Saint Francis, too, though the product of Provençal and northern Italian culture, as a Nazarite. The saint's reputation for self-denial lent itself to this interpretation, while his mystical experiences suggested a connection to the Castilian branch of the Nazarene's religion, a branch known for ascetic and visionary saints that include Teresa of Avila and John of the Cross.[12]

When writing about penitence—the form of asceticism that Chávez felt was most Nazarite/Castilian/Franciscan/New Mexican—he used a specific, limited definition. Among both Franciscans and Spaniards there was self-flagellation, but, he insisted, no public displays of "bloody carnage." Scourging oneself, he argued, was an individual's effort to express his contrition and make right his relationship with God; it was not a cult to suffering and death. Chávez conceded, however, that among Franciscans "more saintly or else overzealous individuals did whip their backs to blood in the privacy of their cells, and this was for long regarded as an outstanding sign of saintliness."[13]

Chávez always attributed the bloody, less appealing side of the *penitente* brotherhoods to Indian influence. Thus his "*penitente* land" is penitential, but its Spanish traditions are not faithfully represented by the well-known New Mexican *penitentes*. One cannot help wondering whether it might be more probable that related tendencies in the Native American and Spanish religious traditions converged to produce the popularity of the brotherhoods. But Chávez preferred to distance himself from the *penitentes* rather than admit what he considered an unworthy element into his Spanish spiritual heritage.[14]

The whole search for national ways of being—as in the idea of the French or German soul—was a late-Romantic concept that Chávez found in Miguel de

Unamuno, pioneering existentialist philosopher, poet, and novelist. Chávez saw Spanish thinking as basically Semitic and so, in his view, lacking in the logical approach to the world characteristic of Greece and all of western Europe except Spain. For him, as for Unamuno, truth is intuitive, essentially emotional and existing in the service of life. Chávez, like the existentialists, considered pure reason less lifegiving than faith and commitment to a worthy cause, and both of these are made easier for the individual by a strengthening tradition. In his short stories there are miracles, but in an ambiguous context that suggests they have happened only in the minds of believers. It is the usefulness of Christian belief, not its absolute truth, that is discreetly conveyed.[15] While Chávez never stated that his faith had become a matter of emotion and commitment rather than reason, he identified his approach to truth by calling himself a Spaniard at heart, that is, more intuitive than strictly rational. Insight comes to Spaniards, he affirmed, in a way related to how a visual artist such as himself experiences truth: "Here in the Castilian atmosphere . . . truth and *hesed* [the Hebrew word for intense love between God and people] are not stated in logical propositions . . . but are seen sharp-edged in the stark figures marching across their naked native countryside." In harmony with this visual/intuitive orientation, the adjectives Chávez used to define all things authentically Spanish are "sad, dry, severe, real."[16]

The idea of New Mexican life as radically different from that of Anglo America, of a separate world revolving around a different, more religious view of existence, also allowed Chávez to respond to another common source of humiliation: criticism of Hispanics for not working hard enough. He asserted that in New Mexico the work ethic was not dominant because of the "eternity-fixed pastoral outlook of the great Castilian plateau."[17] The basic message in this phrase is that Hispanic New Mexicans have their own concerns, very possibly superior to those of the self-righteous Anglos.

New Mexico had retained into the twentieth century, he argued, a special character, which he called pastoral or patriarchal, by virtue of its isolation from non-Castilian/Palestinian influences. With his customary poetic eloquence, he found parallels between biblical/Castilian shepherds and New Mexican stockmen. In an effort to provide scientific credibility for his view, he pointed to similarities in terrain and climate among all three parts of the world.[18] Arid uplands, not lush river valleys, have always been more useful for God's purposes, he argued, since in them nomadic shepherds have the leisure to look and listen for divine guidance under a big sky but are not materially comfortable enough to devote themselves to the pleasures of the flesh.

He bolsters this geographic approach with a Semitic element—patriarchal and monotheistic—in Spanish culture. In addition to the Jews who lived in Spain during the Middle Ages, many of whom stayed on as converts after the expulsion of 1492, Phoenician and Carthaginian settlers are all cited as factors in the creation of the Spanish people's essentially biblical character.

Not that the Hebrew/Castilian patriarchal stock raisers were entirely admirable, Chávez admits. They were accustomed to unrestrained displays of power and treating women as property. The result in Spain, he admits in honesty to himself and the reader, has been machismo and a persistent tension between anarchy and oligarchy. But for Chávez these qualities are merely unfortunate side effects of a valuable lifestyle that makes God's presence luminously perceptible. Again we encounter a pragmatic acceptance of shortcomings in Spanish culture motivated by Chávez's drive to validate what he considered to be his heritage. Or rather, all of his heritage that he chose to recognize, as his careful differentiation between Spanish New Mexicans, *genízaros* (Christianized native peoples), and Mexicans makes clear. Chávez denied that the sixteenth- and seventeenth-century settlers mixed with Native American cultures and gene pools to any significant degree.[19] As a result, when *genízaros* became an important part of New Mexican society in the eighteenth century they were assimilated, he felt, into a thoroughly Spanish culture.

Such a view has been found among "Spanish" New Mexicans for generations. It has roots within Chávez's own family ("my mother always insisted that we were Spanish and not Mexican"[20]) and politics: "At the Constitutional Convention in Cádiz in 1811, Pedro Baustista Pino affirmed with typical New Mexican pride that there was no welter of mixed breeds in New Spain. . . . The inhabitants of New Mexico were either pure Spaniards or pureblooded Indians. . . . He was more or less right in this boast."[21] Chávez himself expressed the wish that Mexico had been called something else, thereby sparing New Mexico confusion with its southern, and very different, neighbor.[22]

In his *Origins of New Mexico Families,* a genealogical monument to the Spanish heritage of New Mexico, Chávez continued his simultaneous disassociation of himself from Native Americans and from Anglo scorn by asserting that it was the *genízaros,* not the descendants of Spaniards, whom the early American travelers and writers called "poor ignorant Mexicans."[23] Still, in his introduction to that voluminous tracing of bloodlines back to Spain, he gave his most balanced assessment of what he identified as his own people. With characteristic good humor he called New Mexican Hispanos' view of themselves one of "some sort of knighted gentry," while their non-Spanish neighbors "believe them to have been nothing but peons and convicts."[24]

His own view, as expressed here, which falls somewhere closer to the heroic than the criminal, blends the truthful with the self-encouraging in an icon few would feel it necessary to quarrel with: "good folks in the main. . . . [We can] picture their fortitude and piety, their constant courage, and a marked sense of idealism."[25] Diego Rivera's idealized images of daily life in Tenochtitlán come to mind, along with the hope that life can, in fact, imitate such art.

NOTES

1. See Padilla's introduction to *The Short Stories of Fray Angélico Chávez* (Albuquerque: University of New Mexico Press, 1987), p. xiii.

2. *Short Stories*, p. 41. Probably the most dramatic condemnation of the aristocracy is woven into the plot and character portrayals of "The Ardent Commandant."

3. Ibid., p. 14.

4. Padilla comments on the negative reaction among Chicano critics to Chávez's pro-Spanish attitude; see ibid., p. xviii.

5. Ibid., p. 34.

6. Ibid., p. 5.

7. Ibid., pp. 17–18.

8. Fray Angélico Chávez, *My Penitente Land* (Albuquerque: University of New Mexico Press, 1974), p. 257.

9. Ibid., p. 267.

10. Ibid., p. 69.

11. Ibid., pp. 76–80.

12. Ibid., p. 107.

13. Ibid., p. 109.

14. A scorn for such contradictions, subordinated to the grander purposes of his larger vision, was also characteristic of Unamuno, the Spanish writer who exerted the most influence on Chávez. As Chávez himself attested, the Spaniard's essays on the "*ánima hispánica,*" the "Spanish soul," struck a resonant chord within him.

15. It would be strange if Unamuno's famous short novel on this theme, *San Manuel Bueno, Mártir* (*St. Manuel the Good, Martyr*) should have left no mark on Chávez's thinking. The protagonist, like Chávez himself for many years, is a well-educated priest serving a remote, traditional village. Unamuno's character has lost his faith in the afterlife but dedicates himself to keeping alive in others old religious beliefs, the most valuable part of the people's culture.

16. For a fuller description of Chávez's sense of the Spanish way of thinking, see *My Penitente Land,* p. 126.

17. Ibid., p. 128.

18. Ibid., p. 8.

19. Ibid., p. 192.

20. Ibid., p. 168.

21. Ibid., p. 223.

22. Ibid., p. 232.

23. Fray Angélico Chávez, *Origins of New Mexico Families: A Genealogy of the Spanish Colonial Period,* rev. ed. (Santa Fe: Museum of New Mexico Press, 1992), p. xviii n1.

24. Ibid., p. xviii.

25. Ibid., p. xix.

PART 3

THE LIFE OF A FRANCISCAN

CHAPTER EIGHT

FRAY ANGÉLICO CHÁVEZ:
The Roots of Franciscan Priesthood

JACK CLARK ROBINSON, O.F.M.
Casa Rivo Torto, Los Lunas, New Mexico

I am not a professional historian or artist, nor a professional writer or literary critic. If I have a profession, it is that I am a professed member of the Order of Friars Minor, the Franciscans, and an ordained priest of the Roman Catholic Church. I cannot speak about Fray Angélico Chávez as a professional historian, artist, writer, or critic, but then neither could Angélico himself have spoken as a professional historian or artist, as a professional writer or professional critic, though certainly he was at one time or another paid for all of those activities, and his level of accomplishment in all of those areas was also certainly in keeping with the highest professional standards. But by profession Fray Angélico Chávez was a member of the Order of Friars Minor and a Roman Catholic priest.

In order to appreciate and understand Fray Angélico's work as a historian, artist, writer, and critic, it is necessary first to see him in the context of his profession and to have some idea of what that profession meant to him and what that profession meant in the world in which he lived and worked.

Manuel Ezequiel Chávez, son of Fabián Chávez and Nicolosa Roybal, born on April 10, 1910, was baptized on May 14, 1910, according to the rite of the Roman Catholic Church, in Saint Clare Church, Wagon Mound, New Mexico. In that time and place there were a number of certainties about the Roman Catholic priests who served the far-flung parishes of the Archdiocese of Santa Fe. First, many of the priests were foreign, mostly French and Belgian, and therefore exotic in the minds of the native New Mexicans, who were primarily of Hispanic and Native American descent. The priest who performed the ceremony of baptism for Manuel was the Reverend Maurice Olier.[1] Second, the priests were generally among the most traveled and best educated members of the community; they were seen as sophisticated and cosmopolitan. They spoke Latin as if they knew what they were saying. Third, priests were seen as men who lived lives of self-sacrifice for the sake of God and others, so they were owed respect and reverence. Finally, the priests were perceived as those who were "close to God," who "talked to God," and who were "about holy things," most especially the sacraments of the Roman Catholic Church. Perhaps this aspect of priesthood was best captured by the teenage Manuel Chávez in a short verse entitled "The Priesthood":

> God drew me out of nothing
> And held me in His hands;
> He draws me out of nothing—
> I hold Him in my hand.[2]

These attitudes toward priests were much the same when the young Manuel and his family moved to Mora, New Mexico, from Wagon Mound, after a brief sojourn in California, and then on to Santa Fe.[3] In Mora, where he attended public school staffed by the religious Sisters of Loretto, Manuel started to read everything that he could about the history of New Mexico, and everything that he read emphasized the contributions of the Franciscans to its early history.[4] Young Manuel's family moved to Santa Fe only three years after the return of the Franciscans to the city in 1921 to staff the cathedral. The Franciscans had been absent from the city for more than seventy-five years when, in May 1919, Albert Thomas Daeger, a Franciscan, became the sixth archbishop of Santa Fe. The archbishop was able to staff Saint Francis Cathedral as well as other parishes in northern New Mexico with his brother Franciscans. Suddenly, those colorful brown-robed figures whom the curious young boy had only read about in history books came to life around him. The results were almost predictable. On August 9, 1924, at age fourteen, Manuel Ezequiel Chávez applied to attend the high-school seminary of the Franciscans in Cincinnati, the first stage of preparation for religious life and priesthood that had also been taken by the Franciscans he knew in Santa Fe.[5]

If the Roman Catholic priesthood in general in northern New Mexico was composed of men who were seen as exotic, sophisticated, close to God, and worthy of reverence, then the Franciscans were seen as all of these things, with some colorful highlights added to the picture by the special nature of their religious community. Francis of Assisi was a medieval Italian mystic who had founded three different communities within the Roman Catholic Church, inspiring as many as five thousand men in his own lifetime to follow him into a life of poverty, chastity, and obedience. Once he was asked to describe the ideal Friar Minor, or member of his own religious community, and Francis replied:

A good Friar Minor should imitate the lives and possess the merits of these holy friars: the perfect faith and love of poverty of Brother Bernard; the simplicity and purity of Brother Leo, . . . the courtesy of Brother Angelo, . . . the gracious look and natural good sense of Brother Masseo, together with his noble and devout eloquence; the mind up-raised to God, possessed in its highest perfection by Brother Giles; the virtuous and constant prayer of Brother Rufino, . . . the patience of Brother Juniper, . . . the bodily and spiritual courage of Brother John of Lauds, . . . the charity of Brother Roger, . . . [and] the caution of Brother Lucidus.[6]

In Franciscan tradition, no one friar defined membership in the community, but instead there is room for a great deal of originality and individuality. No doubt, that breathing room among the friars was appealing to the budding artist in Manuel Ezequiel Chávez as he headed off to Cincinnati in the fall of 1924.

Saint Francis Seraphic Seminary, newly built in the rolling hills of suburban Cincinnati amidst a thick forest of broad-leafed deciduous trees and on an ocean of thick green grass, must have seemed like a foreign planet to the young boy from New Mexico, thrown in with equally wide-eyed boys from the farms of Kansas, the cities of the Ohio River Valley, and the Upper Peninsula of northern Michigan. The educational system that these twenty or so teenagers entered would keep them together in an extraordinary way for most of the next thirteen years. Their lives would be highly regimented, with set times for rising, bathing, eating, exercise, classes, recreation, homework, going to bed, and, of course, prayer. It was a closed system with very little contact with the "outside" world.

Manuel was the only member of his class from New Mexico, and, given the distance, means, and expense of travel, it is to be doubted that Manuel returned to his home state, except for summer vacations, during his high-school career. Instead, he would have taken vacation time with one or the other of his classmates, or remained at the seminary. During one vacation period, Manuel and one of his high-school seminary classmates "borrowed" a car and took a ride to a far part of town called Coryville. They picked up two girls for the afternoon, one of them having a brother who was with the friars. According to Angélico years later, they didn't really do anything sinful: "I doubt that we even kissed them, though if it had been now a days, who knows what would have happened."[7] But Angélico thought years later of reminding this classmate of the incident when that classmate had been elected provincial minister of the friars and was upset that Angélico had done something that was causing "scandal."

The seminary boys' teachers were mostly friar priests, who became surrogate parents as well as role models. The education was extremely good, not narrow, but broad with a focused purpose. Languages, including Latin, were emphasized, and high expectations were placed on the boys, not only in mastery of language but also in creative writing and oral recitation. In turn, they were given a great deal of individualized attention. The closed nature of the system created a reliance on one another for companionship and entertainment. Participation in plays, skits, choral and instrumental music groups as well as a variety of sports and athletic activities was a regular part of every seminarian's life, not only in high school but throughout the thirteen years of training.

In this atmosphere, native artistic, dramatic, and literary talent had an incredible opportunity to flower, and in Manuel all three came to the fore, as exemplified by one notation in the *Brown and White,* a periodical published by the students of the high-school seminary, noting performance of an original three-act drama based on Lord Byron's "Prisoner of Chillon," by Manuel Chávez: "The play was acted and directed by third class students; so magnificent were the lighting effects, so beautiful was the music, so careful and discriminating was the acting, that we feel no hesitation in saying that it displayed high artistic ability."[8] It was about this time that the rector of the seminary, Urban Freundt, O.F.M., first nicknamed Manuel "Angélico," after the medieval artist and in honor of the young man's artistic ability.[9]

During his high-school years Manuel would make over forty contributions to the *Brown and White* and serve as its editor.[10] His contributions would range from humorous, lyric poetry to attempts to examine serious religious themes, such as can be glimpsed in this work published when Manuel was only sixteen years old:

The Friar's Christmas Gift

> With stainless hands the whirling snows
> Have laid an ermine veil;
> A starlight sheen from heaven glows
> To brighten hill and dale.
> Sweet-tonguéd chimes from cloister tower
> Ring in the joyous morn.
> Begins the Mass at midnight hour,
> The eve when Christ was born.

An infirm novice keeps his cell,
Too weak his limbs to raise;
While in his soul the ringing bell
Stirs songs of love and praise.
"As these white snows divinely shine
Against this inky night;
So gleams Thy presence, Lord, near mine,
All radiant, dazzling bright;
As these gray walls are guarded sure
The earth's unspotted gown,
So hast Thou, Lord, my soul kept pure
In this dear tunic brown.
My God! Roll Heaven's gates aside,
And send Thy Son to earth;
Ah, close them not, but ope them wide
For my immortal birth!"
The priest low o'er the altar bends,
The words their message give;
The gates roll back and Christ descends
Again with men to live.
The gates close not, while angels fair
Singing the birth of Love,
With joy the friar's soul now bear
Beyond the gates above.
God in the novice, the novice in Him,
Sublime, eternal Feast.
Among the Saints and Seraphim
The Offering and the Priest!

M.E. Chávez, '29.[11]

Twice in the forty years before Manuel wrote this poem a young novice had been allowed to make profession as a friar just before dying, one of those on December 27.[12] Another young cleric had died on Christmas Eve in the 1880s.[13] Manuel's romantic mind was already at work weaving together history and art, even though the art might draw heavily on the typical teenage fascination with death. But the poem also reflects an appreciation of theological ideas that came to be part of the very air around the Franciscans in training, as well as a foretaste of an entire life spent bringing art and history to the service of faith.

The minor seminary where Manuel Chávez spent most of his teenage years was only the first step in the formation of a Franciscan priest. He entered the novitiate, the second stage of formation, on August 15, 1929. On that day he would have been clothed with a Franciscan habit for the first time and given the name by which he would be known forever afterwards. Each new novice was asked to present three names, one of which would usually then be chosen to represent his new life in religion. Undoubtedly, following up on his high-school nickname, Manuel Chávez would have suggested Angelico for himself. The famous Italian artist of the fourteenth and fifteenth centuries, Fra Angelico was actually a Dominican and not a Franciscan, so officially, when the young novice friar received his new name, it was in honor of a relatively unknown early companion of Saint Francis of Assisi named Angelico. Three years later, Angélico discovered a technical flaw in his religious name and wrote to the provincial minister[14] seeking help. Ironically, the provincial minister then was the very same friar who had, as a high-school seminary teacher, first dubbed the young man Angelico:

> Dear Father Provincial:
> I find that the Friar Minor after whom I am named (Angelico) is not even a "Beatus." Neither is the famous Dominican artist. Hence, it seems as though I have no real Patron Saint.
> Since Father Claude is preparing the new schematismus, I asked him if I could take as my patron *Our Lady of the Angels*; i.e., Portiuncula Day, Aug. 2. For the Blessed Virgin is the best Patron possible, you know. Of course, I intend to keep my name "Angélico." After consulting Fathers Rudolph and Romuald, Fr. Claude told me that it is all right, provided that you grant your permission. And this I humbly ask of you.
> Yours in St. Francis,
> s/frater Angélico Chávez, ofm[15]

The provincial minister gave permission for Angélico to keep his name and to celebrate August 2 as his name's day.

After the novitiate, which would have concluded for Fray Angélico with the first profession of vows as a Franciscan on August 16, 1930, a year and a day after entry, the young friar, along with his classmates, left Cincinnati, where all of their formation had so far taken place, for Detroit. In Detroit, they entered Duns Scotus College, a brand-new school run entirely by the Franciscans of Saint John the Baptist Province and named for the Franciscan philosopher John Duns Scotus. Once again the young friars pursued a broad liberal arts education, though with a heavy concentration in philosophy. Angélico did very well academically in college, most of the time keeping his grades in the "90s," though he did score a "65" and a "68" in chemistry.[16] It was here, in the chapel of Duns Scotus College, that Angélico Chávez made his solemn, or lifetime, profession of the vows of poverty, chastity, and obedience as a Franciscan friar at 9:45 A.M. on August 16, 1933, into the hands of the provincial minister, the Very Reverend Maurice Ripperger.[17]

At Duns Scotus College Angélico began a compilation of thoughts and reflections on the principal feasts of Christ, the Blessed Mother, and the great Franciscan saints. This work would be published as *Seraphic Days* in 1940. At Fray Angélico's request it was not directly attributed to him at the time of publication, but rather the title page said, "Edited from a Friar's Manuscript by Father Sebastian Erbacher, O.F.M." Father Sebastian had been one of Fray Angélico's professors, and in his foreword he describes the work this way:

> When the author of these pages entered upon the study of philosophy as a cleric, he was deeply impressed by the spontaneity and the simplicity of the affective prayer of St. Francis and his early followers. He read and reread the writings of St. Francis, the *Fioretti,* and studied St. Bonaventure, to imbue himself with their spirit. It became his secret desire to compose a series of Franciscan meditations in the style of our Seraphic Father and of the Seraphic Doctor, appealing more to the heart than to the mind. He would make use of sensible things, the creatures of God, to raise the soul to spiritual realities, to God Himself. He would strive to convey his thoughts and express his affections in the language of Holy Writ, without attempting exact quotation, for it was a book of prayer and not of science that was contemplated. . . . The thoughts suggested by the feast of the day moved his heart to speak to God in a personal and simple manner. It was not so much his intention at the time to write a book for others as to force himself to take mental prayer more seriously and to make greater spiritual progress. This personal note prompts the author to hide his identity.[18]

Fray Angélico did make spiritual progress and, after completing his studies of philosophy in Detroit, went on to Oldenburg, Indiana, the home of theology studies for the Franciscans of Saint John the Baptist Province. By spring 1937 those theology studies were completed, and Fray Angélico requested to return to his beloved New Mexico for ordination to the priesthood, instead of being ordained with his classmates in Indiana. This request was granted, making possible his ordination to the priesthood in Saint Francis Cathedral in Santa Fe on May 6, 1937. No doubt, in Fray Angélico's mind and in the minds of his family and many of those in attendance, all of his life led up to the moment when Archbishop Rudolph Gerken, who had succeeded the Franciscan Albert Daeger as archbishop of Santa Fe after the latter's untimely accidental

Figure 8.1 Fray Angélico Chávez, 1937 (courtesy of the Franciscan Archives, Cincinnati)

death in December 1932, imposed his hands on Fray Angélico Chávez and invoked the Holy Spirit to ordain him a priest in the ancient rite of the Church.

Fray Angélico's first priestly assignment, from 1937 until 1943, was Peña Blanca, New Mexico, a parish that included the Spanish missions of Sile, Domingo Station, Cerrillos, and La Bajada, along with the Indian pueblos of Cochiti, Santo Domingo, and San Felipe. In his six years at Peña Blanca, Angélico baptized over 450 children and presided at over forty weddings, and along with the births and weddings there were anointings, burials, confessions, and Communions.[19] It was the work of a missionary priest in those days. Often, this work involved long hours and hard travel between missions, sometimes with seemingly little reward. When Angélico returned to Peña Blanca from the missions, his labors did not cease, but instead he sought to proclaim the gospel in other ways—through his writing, which at this time was still very much poetry and fiction, and through his artwork, including the famous lost *Stations of the Cross* in the ill-fated parish church.

The listing of Fray Angélico's priestly assignments is relatively simple. From 1937 until 1943 he was a missionary in Peña Blanca; from 1943 until 1946, he served as an army chaplain, making two beach head landings with troops in the Pacific Theater in World War II; for two years after his return from the army, Angélico was listed as a mission band member living with the friars at Saint Francis Cathedral in Santa Fe. Then in 1948 he returned to Peña Blanca, where he stayed until he returned to the army in 1951, after being notified that he would be reactivated in 1950.[20] Just before Fray Angélico's second assignment to Peña Blanca, he wrote a letter to the provincial minister outlining the approach he would like to take to the mission work if reassigned to Peña Blanca. The letter reveals much of what was in his heart concerning his work as a missionary friar, as well as some of the common language and attitudes of the day regarding Indians:

June 12, 1948

A couple of weeks ago I preached at the First Mass of a Cochiti Spanish-American boy whom I sent to the diocesan Seminary ten years ago. The Indians were so glad to see me and begged me to come back to them. At the same time I noticed a resurgence of faith among them, largely because of the first Cochiti priest and his first Mass. Many have left their pagan ways. I made the most of it in my sermon. Now I think is the time to catch opportunity by the forelock. And so I offer myself as resident missionary in Cochiti.

There is no place for the Padre there, no convenience at all, except a little room by the sacristy where I could sleep until I made the Indians build me a couple of rooms next to the church this summer. I could take my meals at the home of the new priest's parents, who run the Pueblo grocery store nearby. Besides Cochiti, I could take care of Sile on that side of the river [the Rio Grande]. Then there would be need of two priests only at Peña Blanca.

My idea is to make the whole Pueblo Catholic by living with the Indians, especially now that their spirit is as good as never before. At the same time I want to make the experiment of living like a real Franciscan, just with the barest essentials. Am not even asking for a car. In the meantime I can do a lot of writing from material I have collected so far; and within a year I can come to Santa Fe or Albuquerque for more manuscript material as I need it.

I think this course would make me perfectly happy, in that I don't feel well being just a bookworm priest. I'll continue doing this, of course, but at the same time trying to go back to a real primitive Franciscan life for the good of my soul and, if God wills, an example for future work in the other Pueblos.

If you or the Chapter [i.e., provincial chapter, the highest elected governing body] think my idea is wacky, then scrap it. But I am confident in it and not ashamed in the least.

In St. Francis,

s/fr. Angélico[21]

It does not appear that Fray Angélico was allowed to pursue this particular mission strategy, as he lived in the friars' house in Peña Blanca when he was transferred there in 1948, though he was assigned as the missionary to Cochiti Pueblo and the Spanish village of Sile. But this time in Peña Blanca was to be relatively brief, as Fray Angélico was called back to the army in the summer of 1950, returned to active duty in 1951, and stayed with the army through the three years of the Korean conflict. But instead of being sent to Asia, he was sent to Europe and was able to make contacts with European and especially Spanish culture that would prove valuable for his later historical research.

When Fray Angélico returned from the army in the summer of 1953, he was assigned by his religious superiors as an associate at Jémez Pueblo. This mission of the Franciscans included the Indian pueblos of Jémez, Zía, and Santa Ana, as well as the Spanish villages of San Isidro, Cañon, and Ponderosa. At Ponderosa, Angélico was intrigued to find that the village church was dedicated to Santo Toribio, the only one in New Mexico dedicated to this missionary bishop saint of Lima, Peru; once again wedding art and faith, Angélico saw to the restoration by E. Boyd of the little santo of the saint that was the prized possession of the community of Ponderosa.[22]

A year later, while still assigned to Jémez Pueblo, Fray Angélico undertook an incredible mission work that carried him throughout the state. Always fascinated and devoted to the Blessed Mother of Christ under the title of *La Conquistadora,* the little image of Mary that had been brought to New Mexico by Spanish friars in the 1600s, Fray Angélico had written three books and numerous articles detailing her story.[23] On May 2, 1954, he began a pilgrimage with the little statue that took them to ninety-five churches, where he preached eighty-five sermons, and they took part in eighty-two processions, concluding on September 5.[24] It was an enormous effort to evangelize, to "make use of sensible things, the creatures of God, to raise the soul to the spiritual realities, to God Himself."[25] During the time at Jémez Pueblo, Fray Angélico also began his great work with the archives of the Archdiocese of Santa Fe, taking material with him to the pueblo to review its content and publishing the results in 1957.

In 1959 Fray Angélico began the one part of his priestly career that he would later in a sense deny. He was sent as the missionary to Cerrillos, New Mexico. He was pastor of a parish, something he had no real interest in being, for he knew that a pastor faced administrative responsibilities as well as the sacramental duties that every priest has. In 1993, Fray Angélico told me, "My vision of being a Franciscan is Saint Francis. Somewhere I learned that Francis was never really minister general of the order, but Brother Leo was. What Francis wanted to do was to write his songs. I am proud that I was never a pastor or guardian or superior of any sort, but rather I was a writer, just like Francis."[26] This sojourn into the world of being an administrator as well as a priest and friar lasted until 1964, when Fray Angélico was stationed briefly at Holy Family Friary in Albuquerque, then moved to Peña Blanca, where he lived for seven years. At both Holy Family and Peña Blanca, Fray Angélico's official assignment was writing and research.

The end of Fray Angélico's time in Cerrillos, the brief stay in Albuquerque, and the return to Peña Blanca coincided with one of the greatest events in the twentieth-century history of the Roman Catholic Church, the Second Council of the Vatican, generally referred to as Vatican II. This ecumenical council, or meeting of all of the Roman Catholic bishops of the world, along with representatives of other Christian bodies, has had a profound impact on every aspect of the life of the Church since. The image of priesthood, the language and shape of the sacraments, and the idea of what the Church is itself have all changed as a result of this two-year-long council.

The council seems to have had a powerful, if delayed, impact on Fray Angélico. Exactly what led up to the events in his life of 1971 and the eighteen years that followed is unclear, but the beginning of that momentous period was described this way in a letter of the provincial minister of Saint John the Baptist Province:

On the morning of June 30, 1971, Father Angélico's superior at our Friary in Peña Blanca, New Mexico telephoned me to say that Angélico had left early that morning in his automobile, taking with him all of "his books and other possessions." He had said nothing about leaving, other than a remark some weeks previously that he "would be gone in about a month." The statement at the time was attributed simply to irritation and nervousness since he was then suffering acutely from a severe dental problem. Before his departure, he left a note on the bulletin board reading: "I shall have left the Order and the Church."[27]

Fray Angélico was one of many, many priests and religious men and women in the United States who "left" in the ten years or so after the full impact of Vatican II began to set in. Some left because the changes came too fast, others because the changes seemed to come too slowly, and still others because they were not certain as to where the changes left them.

At the time of Fray Angélico's departure, the provincial minister of Saint John the Baptist Province happened to be a canonist, or Church lawyer, of German descent. Until the end of this man's term as provincial minister, he periodically sent Angélico money and persisted in trying to get Fray Angélico to sign the application for a formal dispensation from his vows as a Franciscan.[28] Angélico never sent back the signed forms or the money.

Angélico's very personal decision, to neither formally leave nor physically return, may have eventually served him and those who admire him well. Archbishop James Peter Davis, like the provincial minister in Cincinnati, had wanted an "administrative dismissal" for Angélico, but when the Most Reverend Robert Sánchez became archbishop in 1974, his first appointment was to name Fray Angélico the official archivist of the Archdiocese. Archbishop Sánchez also reached out to Fray Angélico in other ways:

Through his kindness, concern and friendship, Archbishop Sánchez led Father Angélico to reconciliation with the Church. On several previous occasions, Archbishop Sánchez encouraged Father Angélico to concelebrate with him, to again make whole his person and by the public concelebration repair whatever scandal may have been given by Angélico in divorcing himself from the Church. Therefore, on Christmas eve, having reconciled with the Father, Father Angélico concelebrated Mass.

Father Angélico is now in good standing as a priest. He is not in active ministry but he is in good standing. However, as you know from the Constitutions, Father Angélico is no longer a formal member of the Franciscan Order. But he will always remain a Franciscan at heart and we have no objection to his pen name of Fray Angélico Chávez.[29]

"He will always remain a Franciscan at heart."[30] Indeed, Fray Angélico did remain a Franciscan. The order may have technically dismissed him, but when he decided to come home in 1989 there was certainly a place for him. Father Crispin Butz, then the rector of the cathedral and the head of the local Franciscan community, worked with Fray Angélico to facilitate his return to the friars, and about December 1, 1989, Angélico moved into Saint Francis Friary, making a full circle to return to the place where, sixty-five years before, the friars had sent fourteen-year-old Manuel Chávez off to become what he would always be, no matter what avocations he may have pursued, a Franciscan friar and a priest.

Much of this essay is the result of research which I was able to do in the Cincinnati archives of the Province of Saint John the Baptist of the Order of Friars Minor and in the records of San Diego Mission in Jémez Pueblo and Our Lady of Guadalupe Parish in Peña Blanca. Much of it also comes from my personal experience of seventeen years with the Franciscans, where I have had the privilege of being a novice in the very same novitiate house where Fray Angélico was a novice and, since then, of living for eight years in three of the Franciscan houses where Fray Angélico lived so long, Holy Family Friary in Albuquerque, San Diego Friary in Jémez Pueblo, and Our Lady of Guadalupe Friary in Peña Blanca, all in New Mexico. It is my sincere wish that what I have said may help the reader understand that who Fray Angélico was as a Franciscan and as a priest had a remarkable effect on everything else that he did. His life was lived in pursuit of the highest of Franciscan ideals—to proclaim the gospel of Jesus Christ by whatever means were available, whether they were the pulpit, the artist's palette, the poet's words, or the historian's search for truth.

NOTES

1. Information taken from a baptismal certificate found in the archives of Saint John the Baptist Province of the Order of Friars Minor in Cincinnati, in the file for Angélico Chávez. Hereafter "Archives, SJBP-OFM."

2. Manuel E. Chávez, "The Priesthood," *Brown and White* 5, no. 5 (Feb 1929), p. 1. The *Brown and White* was the school magazine of Saint Francis Seraphic Seminary, Cincinnati, during the time that Manuel Chávez was a student of the seminary.

3. Interview with Fray Angélico Chávez, March 4, 1993, Saint Francis Cathedral Friary, Santa Fe.

4. See Robert Huber, "Fray Angélico Chávez, 20th-Century Renaissance Man," *New Mexico* Magazine 48, no. 3–4 (Mar./Apr.1970), pp. 18–23, 48.

5. Archives, SJBP-OFM.

6. Marion A. Habig, ed. and trans., *St. Francis of Assisi—Omnibus of Sources* (Chicago: Franciscan Herald Press, 1973). p. 1218. This quotation is from a small thirteenth- or fourteenth-century work here compiled in an omnibus. The work is commonly known as *The Mirror of Perfection,* and the quotation is from paragraph 85 of the critical text.

7. Interview with Fray Angélico Chávez, March 4, 1993, Saint Francis Cathedral Friary, Santa Fe.

8. "The Month's News," *Brown and White* 3, no. 3 (Dec. 1926), p. 5.

9. Interview with Fray Angélico Chávez, March 4, 1993, Saint Francis Cathedral Friary, Santa Fe.

10. Archives, SJBP-OFM.

11. Manuel E. Chávez, "The Friar's Christmas Gift," *Brown and White* 3, no. 3 (Dec. 1926), p. 6.

12. *The Franciscans 1859–1979: The Province of St. John the Baptist, Cincinnati, Ohio* (Cincinnati: Saint John the Baptist Province of the Order of Friars Minor, 1979), p. 160.

13. George Hellman, O.F.M., *Necrology of the Friars of St. John the Baptist Province, Cincinnati, Ohio and of the Missionaries from St. Leopold Province, Tyrol* (Cincinnati: Saint John the Baptist Province of the Order of Friars Minor, 1989).

14. All around the world, Franciscans are divided into groups called provinces. During most of Fray Angélico Chávez's lifetime there were six Franciscan provinces in the United States. As these provinces grew, they did not always adhere to any geographical logic. Thus, the Province of Saint John the Baptist, though headquartered in Cincinnati, included missions in northern New Mexico and Arizona; similarly, the Province of the Sacred Heart of Jesus was headquartered in Saint Louis but included missions in southern Arizona and New Mexico. The "minister and servant" of all of the Franciscan friars of a particular province is referred to variously as the provincial minister or the minister provincial. Familiarly, Franciscans refer to this office holder as "father provincial," "the provincial," or even "the pro."

15. Fray Angélico Chávez to Urban Freundt, Oct. 21, 1932, letter in Archives, SJBP-OFM.

16. Archives, SJPB-OFM.

17. Ibid.

18. Sebastian Erbacher, O.F.M., foreword to *Seraphic Days* (by Fray Angélico Chávez) (Paterson, N.J.: St. Anthony Guild Press, 1940), pp. iii–iv.

19. Parish records (*Baptismal Register, Marriage Register, Communion Register,* and *Book of the Dead*), Our Lady of Guadalupe Parish, Peña Blanca, New Mexico.

20. Archives, SJBP-OFM.

21. Fray Angélico Chávez to Romuald Mollaun, June 12, 1948, letter in Archives, SJBP-OFM.

22. E. Boyd, "The Only Bulto of Santo Toribio," *El Palacio* 64, no.3–4 (Mar.–Apr. 1957), pp. 109–14.

23. Fray Angélico Chávez, *Our Lady of the Conquest* (Santa Fe: Historical Society of New Mexico, 1948); and Chávez, *La Conquistadora: The Autobiography of an Ancient Statue* (Paterson, N.J.: St. Anthony Guild Press, 1954).

24. Archives, SJBP-OFM.

25. Erbacher, *Seraphic Days*, p. iii.

26. Interview with Fray Angélico Chávez, March 4, 1993, Saint Francis Cathedral Friary, Santa Fe. I must add that Fray Angélico's comment that Saint Francis was never minister general of the order is no more accurate than his recollection that he himself had never been a pastor. Saint Francis was the first minister general of the order, though Francis is quoted as always saying that the Holy Spirit was the true minister general of the order.

27. Roger Huser, O.F.M., to Constantine Koser, O.F.M., August 13, 1974, letter in Archives, SJBP-OFM.

28. Archives, SJBP-OFM.

29. Andrew Fox, O.F.M., to Reynaldo Rivera, O.F.M., July 8, 1977, letter in Archives, SJBP-OFM.

30. Ibid.

CHAPTER NINE

THE SAINT FRANCIS OF FRAY ANGÉLICO CHÁVEZ

MURRAY BODO, O.F.M.
Thomas More College, Crestview Hills, Kentucky

He began to write in earnest of Saint Francis of Assisi as a high-school student at Saint Francis Seminary in Cincinnati. The young Manuel E. Chávez—his given name prior to receiving "Angélico" as his religious name—wrote poems and, later, editorials for the *Brown and White,* the seminary magazine, that took as their theme the life and spirituality of Saint Francis. Romantic and filled with the enthusiasm of youth, these pieces contained lines such as, "For he sought no hand of mortal, nor the sword of gallant knight, / But the sweet Love-Grail of Jesus; long he wished that blessed sight."[1]

In the years when Fray Angélico was a seminarian, boys who wanted to become Franciscan priests entered the seminary after the eighth grade. And if you were a boy from northern New Mexico, where the Franciscan friars of the Cincinnati Province of Saint John the Baptist ministered, then you had to leave your parents at the tender age of fourteen and travel from New Mexico to Cincinnati to begin studies for the Franciscan priesthood. A boy needed, to be sure, a lot of idealism and love for Saint Francis and Christ to make that extraordinary outer and inner journey; thus the idealism of the lines above, written when Fray Angélico was seventeen years old. Or, as editor of the *Brown and White* in his senior year, this description of Francis in an editorial: "And he loved his God so much, that he devoted his whole life to His Love and to the all-embracing love of his fellowmen in the villages and in the big cities."[2]

It is extraordinary that even at so young an age Fray Angélico captures the very essence of Saint Francis of Assisi's spirituality in the poem and the editorial. The Franciscan scholar Duane V. Lapsanski has defined what Fray Angélico calls Jesus' "Love-Grail" as an "invitation to enter into a new level of existence, one lived completely in God's presence and characterized by a total self-giving to the Father. . . . The surrender must be accompanied by a whole-hearted trust in the Lord as one's helper and savior and must be expressed in deeds of loving service."[3]

In 1932, two years after his novitiate (which followed immediately after the seminarian's senior year of high school) and during his second year of college, Fray Angélico is already beginning to see the stigmatic Saint Francis as the quintessential emblem of the person who has sought and found the Love-Grail of Jesus. In the final stanza of "Stigmata of St. Francis," a poem published in *St. Anthony Messenger,* Fray Angélico writes in the persona of Saint Francis praying at La Verna, the mountain on which he was imprinted with the wounds of Christ: "Dear Christ! At last I scan / La Verna's cliff-veiled side. / Complete the picture You began / And have me crucified!"[4] This poem and the allusion to the stigmata in the 1932 poem "The Son of St. Francis"[5] were surely influenced by Fray Angélico's spiritual formation as a Franciscan friar. What it meant to be a Franciscan would have been constantly in the forefront of his consciousness, for he was still in his temporary vows of poverty, chastity, and obedience, taken for three years at the end of the novitiate year. It was under-stood that though the vows brought inner freedom and intimacy with God, they also involved an inner conformity to the crucified Christ, the emblem of which was the sacred stigmata of Saint Francis.

After professing his temporary vows the young friar then went immediately to the college seminary, Duns Scotus College, in Detroit, where, after his third year in college, he made his profession of solemn vows as a Franciscan friar. He spent his last year of college as a fully professed Franciscan. In that final year of 1933, again in *St. Anthony Messenger,* Fray Angélico published the poem "The City of St. Francis," in which he compares Santa Fe, New Mexico, to Assisi and asserts of Mount Alverno (a variation of Mount La Verna), where Saint Francis received the stigmata: "Why, his dear Alverno / Was the kingly Monte Sol! / And the Seraph—Sun of Zia / Blazoned on a golden scroll!"[6] This poem con-tinues the motif of the stigmata of Saint Francis, but it is also a poem in which the oneiric image of Santa Fe emerges after eight years of Fray Angélico's formation in a German-American milieu. The polarity between his Franciscan formation in Ohio and Michigan (and later in Indiana as a cleric in theological studies) and the roots of his Hispanic heritage in New Mexico will become an ongoing tension in his life and work. At times this tension will cause him to suffer with the crucified Christ a sense of alienation and separation from some of his Franciscan brothers because of their lack of sensitivity to him as a His-panic New Mexican. His parents, too, will be a tension: his surrogate parents, the Franciscan mentors of his formation, versus his biological parents and all they stand for. It is a tension the young Angélico tries too quickly to resolve in "Mother of St. Francis," a facile re-telling of an old Franciscan story. After the porter of Francis's community turns away a friar's mother who has come to beg, Francis instructs him, " 'Sell the book, then, little Brother, / Give her what is paid to you; / For the mother of each friar / Is *my* little Mother, too.' "[7]

But one's parents are not, alas, always accepted so uncritically as in this story. Nor are one's roots ignored completely; at times Fray Angélico felt the sting of prejudice and misunderstanding, even from his brothers, and this served only to confirm his strong conviction that the true following of Saint Francis is a following of Christ that involves misunderstanding and even betrayal by one's own brothers. This suffering is what conforms us to Christ, imprinting on our soul the wounds Saint Francis carried in his body. We experience the tension, the pull of opposing forces, but we continue to walk in the footsteps of Jesus, in search of the Love-Grail.

The conviction that the stigmatic Francis is the culmination of the Christo-centric spirituality of Saint Francis remains deeply embedded in Fray Angélico's soul throughout his years as a friar, as evidenced in his 1965 description of St. Francis' vision: "Francis looked up and saw floating above him what seemed like a great bird of throbbing fire. . . . But instead of two wings, it had six. . . . And all of them had quivering golden flames for feathers. . . . In the midst of those fiery wings Francis saw none else than Jesus Crucified . . . at last he had seen what he had sought so long, the Bird of Perfect Joy."[8] The Bird of Perfect Joy is, of course, the crucified Christ, whom Saint Francis loved from the moment he heard Christ speak from the crucifix of San Damiano, the tumbledown chapel that Francis repaired with his own hands. The Bird of Perfect Joy is *the* image of the Love-Grail, which is internalized so intensely that it becomes manifest on Saint Francis's body. As the scholar Lawrence Cunningham has written, "the early biographers of Francis clearly connect the stigmata to his intense devotion to the crucified Christ."[9]

The Bird of Perfect Joy, in addition to being a symbol of the Love-Grail, is also an allusion to the quintessential Franciscan story of Perfect Joy wherein Francis and Brother Leo are on the road from Perugia to Saint Mary of the Angels on the plain below Assisi. Saint Francis says to Brother Leo:

When we come to Saint Mary of the Angels, soaked by the rain and frozen by the cold, all soiled with mud and suffering from hunger, and we ring at the gate of the Place and the brother porter comes and says angrily: "Who are you?" And we say: "We are two of your brothers." And he contradicts us, saying: "You are not telling the truth. . . . Go away!" And he does not open for us, but makes us stand outside in the snow and rain, cold and hungry, until night falls—then if we endure all those insults and cruel rebuffs patiently, without being troubled and without complaining, and if we reflect humbly and charitably that porter really knows us and that God makes him speak against us, oh, Brother Leo, write that perfect joy is there. . . . Above all the graces and gifts of the Holy Spirit which Christ gives to His friends is that of conquering oneself and willingly enduring sufferings, insults, humiliation, and hardships for the love of Christ.[10]

The Franciscan as the lover of Christ crucified, the Franciscan as one wounded with love for Him who first loved us, is an image that recurs in Fray Angélico's poetry from boyhood to maturity. For example, two of the best poems that appear in his 1939 volume of poetry *Clothed with the Sun* (published two years after his ordination to the priesthood) again explore the stigmata of Saint Francis. In "Marionette," Chávez argues:

> You should be the saint, St. Francis
> Of marionettes, whose every move
> In all their seeming mad-cap dances
> Depends on strings pulled from above.
>
> As in that scene of strange desires,
> When God peered from the mountain's crest
> And lifted you with golden wires
> That pierced your hands and feet and breast.[11]

Here the image is that of Francis as marionette who "depends" (in both meanings: hanging from and depending on) God, whose golden wires pierce Francis's hands and feet and breast in a "scene of strange desires"—strange in what Francis asked in prayer when he journeyed to Mount La Verna to begin a forty-day fast in prayer and solitude, as was his custom, in honor of Saint Michael the Archangel: "My Lord Jesus Christ, I pray You to grant me two graces before I die: the first is that during my life I may feel in my soul and body, as much as possible, that pain which You, dear Jesus, sustained in the hour of Your most bitter Passion. The second is that I may feel in my heart, as much as possible, that excessive love with which You, O Son of God, were inflamed in willingly enduring such suffering for us sinners."[12] Strange to us, so seemingly masochistic a desire, but not strange to one so deeply in love with Christ crucified as was Francis of Assisi.

The second poem, "I Vowed," again focuses on the stigmata and reimagines an image that is contained in the account of the stigmata in *The Little Flowers of St. Francis.* Saint Francis tells Brother Leo that God asked for three gifts, instructing Francis to search in his bosom for the offerings. After finding a large golden coin there and offering it to God, Francis was asked to do so two more times. Francis interprets the miraculous coins he finds to represent the three vows of obedience, poverty, and chastity.[13] Here again, the three vows are intimately connected with the experience of the sacred stigmata. Fray Angélico reimages this scene in the last two lines of "I Vowed": "Behold, the treasures that He pressed / Into my hands are little holes."[14]

Francis the poet inspires Fray Angélico the poet to speak in images: the Bird of Perfect Joy, Marionette, and Little Holes, with the negative/positive valences of an empty hole as a full sharing in the wounds of Christ, themselves negative and positive: wounds, but wounds that also heal and save and give birth to the Church. Always the cross of Our Lord Jesus Christ is figured by Fray Angélico in the Bird of Perfect Joy, the Marionette, and Little Holes; in their metaphorical overtones these images signify both the penetration of the love of Christ into the body of Francis transformed by love into the image of Christ and the emptying Saint Paul writes of in a passage dear to the heart of Saint Francis: "Have this mind among yourselves, which is yours in Christ Jesus, who, though he was in the form of God, did not count equality with God a thing to be grasped, but emptied himself, taking the form of a servant, being born in the likeness of men. And being found in human form he humbled himself and became obedient to death, even death on a cross." (Philippians 2: 5–8)

In "The Singing Tree," the fifth poem in the sequence "The Stigmata of St. Francis" in *Clothed with the Sun,* Fray Angélico casts Francis himself as the tree he saw in one of his dreams, thereby tying the oneiric image of tree to the archetype of tree as a symbol of the desire for ascent to the heavens. But this singing tree, in its desire to ascend to the heights, is struck by lightning, "because of its tall head," its spiritual ambition to be one with the crucified Christ. The ascent becomes the descent, as it was for Christ, who descended to be one of us, who humbled himself, in the words of Saint Paul quoted above; and in descending and dying on the cross, becomes ascent to the Father. For the tree's very felling (the lightning of the wounds of Christ) will be its ascent, "For soon winged lumbermen will heave this rood / Up to the workshop of the Carpenter."[15] The implication is that the real song is the song of the tree's burning, being consumed and felled in the ecstatic love of Christ.

Again and again in his poetry, from the time he was a young high-school seminarian, Fray Angélico draws upon the life of Saint Francis for inspiration. And it is the stigmata of Saint Francis that seem to be the recurrent muse of his Francis poems. He seemed to identify most with Francis's desire to be transformed into the crucified Christ. It is here in this mystical experience that the Franciscan's life finds its consummation. It is the Bird of Perfect Joy that liberates Franciscan spirituality from the Romantic and often sentimental "birdbath" image. The winged thing of Saint Francis' spirituality, as Fray Angélico saw so clearly, is not a pretty little bird, or Francis speaking to the birds (though he did preach to the birds), but a winged seraph that reveals beneath its beautiful six wings the crucified Christ, whose embrace is the final seal upon the Franciscan's quest of the Love-Grail, a quest that begins with Saint Francis' embrace of the Incarnation as the center of his spirituality.

The enfleshment of God in Jesus Christ is *the* mystery that moves Saint Francis to praise. Because of Jesus Christ the whole material universe is holy. Fray Angélico expresses this profound incarnationalism of Saint Francis in his ambitious poem "The Virgin of Port Lligat":

> Praised be the Lord for Brother Sun
> And Sister Moon, for all great things above
> And all small things below that fly or crawl,
> All brethren, we, by amber blood as by His love;
> But most of all for that one Sister Star
> That pointed to a stall
> Where ox and ass one night
> Saw in a wailing Nova how the Word that
> fashioned all,
> By fusing with a maiden's molecules, geared infinite
> To nuclear.[16]

That movement of infinite to nuclear (in the sense of the nucleus of things) is Bethlehem; it is also La Verna and the ecstatic experience of the stigmata as the consummation of Francis' quest for God and God's quest for Francis, where the spiritual becomes incarnate in St. Francis' body, where infinite love becomes the nuclear wounds of Christ, their imprint nucleus of the positively charged love of God incarnate in Saint Francis' soul and body.

NOTES

1. *Brown and White* 4:1 (Oct. 1927), p.3.

2. Ibid., 5:5 (Jan. 1929), p.2.

3. Duane V. Lapsanski, *Evangelical Perfection: An Historical Examination of the Concept in the Early Franciscan Sources* (New York: Franciscan Institute, Saint Bonaventure University, 1977), p. 1.

4. "Stigmata of St. Francis," *St. Anthony Messenger* (Sept. 1932), p. 164.

5. Ibid. (April 1931), p. 489.

6. Ibid. (Sept. 1933), p. 167.

7. Ibid. (Oct. 1937), p. 291.

8. Ibid. (Oct. 1965), p. 36.

9. Lawrence S. Cunningham, "The Strange Stigmata," *Christian History* 42, vol. 13 (1994), No. 2, p. 37.

10. *The Little Flowers of St. Francis, Omnibus of Sources,* ed. Marion A. Habig (Chicago: Franciscan Herald Press), 1973, pp. 1319–20.

11. Fray Angélico Chávez, *Clothed with the Sun* (Santa Fe: Writers' Editions, Inc., 1939), p. 27.

12. *The Little Flowers of St. Francis,* p. 1448.

13. Ibid., pp. 1446–47.

14. Chávez, *Clothed with the Sun,* p. 29.

15. Ibid.

16. Fray Angélico Chávez, *The Virgin of Port Lligat* (Fresno: Academy Library Guild, 1959), vs 82–91, pp. 25–27.

CHAPTER TEN

MEMORIES OF FRAY ANGÉLICO CHÁVEZ

THOMAS E. CHÁVEZ
Palace of the Governors, Santa Fe

The following is an edited and condensed version of a talk given by Thomas E. Chávez on March 21, 1996, three days after the death of his uncle, Fray Angélico Chávez. His presentation was part of a panel on Chávez's work at the joint meeting of the Rocky Mountain and Pacific Coast Councils of Latin American Studies held at the Loretto Inn in Santa Fe.

It's humbling to be asked to speak to this audience of important historians, academics, and family members, and even more difficult with the recent passing of Angélico, although we expected it. He'd been sick for a while, was ready to go, wanted to go, and he did as Saint Francis did—he let himself go. Originally I declined the invitation to speak on this panel for fear that Angélico, my harshest critic, would still be here and would walk in on me! I had the pleasure and the honor not only of knowing the man but of working with him—not as an uncle but as a colleague—and knowing him as a human being and as a priest.

As I listened to a newscast driving home yesterday, I heard about the state legislature's session, the governor's activities, the debate about Indian gambling, and other items. Near the end of the broadcast, there was a brief announcement about the death of Fray Angélico Chávez, with two lines quoted from the *New Mexican,* our local newspaper. This perplexed me. Here was a man who was a great man. *We* lost a great man, not the Church, not Santa Fe, not New Mexico, but everyone lost this person, and he received two lines on the newscast. I rationalized it in this way: Who here remembers who the pope was when Michelangelo died? Who was the king of Spain when Cervantes went to the great library in the sky? Who was the king or queen of England when Shakespeare passed on? Who cares, unless they're very bored? Fifty years from now only a bored person will even care to remember who the governor of New Mexico was when Angélico lived, or that the legislature was grappling in a special session, or that the public debate was about gambling. And until yesterday, people in Albuquerque couldn't even get the news of Angélico's death on television. The death of one of New Mexico's greatest human beings wasn't announced on television. But the *New York Times* has called to ask for details, and they will publish an article on Angélico. We tend to overlook the people in our own backyard.

My story with Angélico began as a youth. I was just a young, towheaded tyke with my dad's haircut; at Angélico's suggestion, Dad stuck a bowl on my hair and cut it. The first story I heard about Angélico was from my father. Angélico baptized me in Saint Francis Cathedral and joked that my name should be changed from Thomas Esteban to Thomas Steve, so that my initials would be T. S. to mean "tough shit." The next great memory I have of him is when my father was sworn in as a judge in Los Angeles. Angélico gave the benediction at the impressive public ceremony and said, "Now, if we could get the pope to cooperate, I'd become an archbishop!" And it was on another of Angélico's trips to California that I had a revelation and got up the courage to tell him about it: "Uncle Pio," I said, using our nickname for him, "I want to be a historian." I thought this was a great thing to say to him.

And he answered, "What for?"

And I had no answer for him. In fact, I still don't, so maybe I learned from him!

One summer I came here to New Mexico and stayed with my aunts and uncles. Angélico would always come to the family house that my grandfather had built on Acequia Madre Street. One weekend he took my brother and me to Cerrillos, where he was stationed. We were twelve and eleven, so we had a better idea what to say to priests—no cuss words! We worked in the garden with him. Being a big baseball fan, I watched the All-Star game on television, and he came inside periodically to ask the scores. He talked a little about working at Golden, which was part of his circuit.

Imagine being a child growing up and someone in your family writes books. Every time he published a book, Angélico would send it to my father, inscribed to my mother and family. To think that someone in my family wrote books! I read his books even though I didn't understand them. I had no inkling what he was writing about, but his books made a big impression on me as a child.

When I moved to Albuquerque, Angélico had retired from the priesthood and got a job under Archbishop Sánchez to work with the archives. I visited him on many occasions. He would drive down to Albuquerque and stay two or three days at a time in the dorms of what was then the University of Albuquerque and work on the archives. This was after he published the book *Archives of the Archdiocese of Santa Fe,* and he was constantly frustrated that everything had been moved around, left in disarray, and that some of the documents were missing. Although that embittered him a little, he was pleased to begin the reorganization himself, and now the archives are in Santa Fe.

My first paper in graduate school for the required historiography course was on the church at Golden, which Angélico had restored. I interviewed him over dinner in an Albuquerque bar (he had a scotch). He told me the whole story about working the pulley to get the adobes up and how his remodeled church had become one of the most photographed in New Mexico. He was proud of that. I met the people of Golden, who had nothing but fond memories of him, because they had helped him to do the church. His granting the interview and giving me information on Golden was the first encouragement I had received from him to be a historian.

When I moved to Santa Fe and became the director at the Palace of the Governors, I saw him almost daily, because he came to work in the History Library. Sometimes I'd interrupt him, but usually he'd volunteer to tell me what he was researching. He would say, "I've got this name I'm looking up," or "Do you recall . . . ?" He knew full well I didn't know it, but it made me feel good because he was a lot smarter than me. Although he never directly congratulated me for my accomplishments at the museum, he would compliment me in his own way. For example, France Scholes had discovered documents in London in 1936 that dated the founding of Santa Fe to 1607 and published an article in 1945 citing these documents. So we retraced the documents and found them in the same place and brought them back to Santa Fe. And Angélico was pleased. When he came to my office, he didn't say "Good job, Tom," but instead, "Do you have the documents here?" Then, "I want you to look at this article I wrote, because there's something that will shed light on them." And when he was happy like that and pleased, there was a twinkle in his eye. And that's all he said and walked out.

He once took me to his apartment on Johnson Street to show me his card catalogue system—how he kept his information. Think of all the books he did. Read the footnotes in some of the translations he did. And think how he did it without a computer. For most of us, it's beyond the realm of imagination anymore. It's like doing math without a calculator. And he let me in on a secret: "I learned this from France Scholes," the stellar New Mexico historian who was his historical mentor.

Once I was to introduce Angélico at a presentation he was making, and I sent over a draft for his approval. He had published *My Penitente Land,* a free-flowing essay, and I commented that he wrote this essay about Hispanic New Mexico before Carlos Fuentes and Octavio Paz ever thought of the form. He knew who they were, of course, but he caught me in the plaza and asked, "Who's Carlos Fuentes and Octavio Paz?"

I started to explain, and he got a twinkle in his eye, so I just said, "Never mind!" He liked to play those games with you.

We brought some hide paintings to Santa Fe from Switzerland that had left New Mexico in the eighteenth century. As usual, Angélico never said "Good job" about the Segesser paintings. But when we had the symposium on the paintings at the Palace of the Governors museum he participated. And without my asking, he submitted an article for a subsequent anthology. Among other items, his article identified who painted the works.

As I started publishing, I gave him copies of my books and he never kept them. He even gave me the research books that he used, translations and journals. He gave them to me with his notations, saying, "I want to give them to you, Tom, to let the devil out the side door," because he knew people would want them for resale because they had value. I use them now in my office. When he returned my books he would say, "The research is good."

As I worked at the museum he would constantly come to visit. He came to see the renovation of the new History Library and looked at the new tile wall. He asked that the ceremony in which he received the Order of Isabel la Católica from the Spanish government be held in the library. And he allowed his photo for *National Geographic* to be taken in the archives there.[1]

And finally, one day came the pinnacle of my career. I might build a new museum or bring collections and paintings back to this country, but the pinnacle of my career was the day he came into my office and said, "Tom, I can't get what's up here [in my mind] down here [to my hands]. It doesn't come out anymore. And so the archbishop has my manuscript on the vicar Juan Felipe Ortiz. I want you to call him and get that manuscript and finish it for me." He could have gone to Southwest historian John Kessell or David Weber or any number of people who were better or more advanced than I. But there could have been no better compliment to me. And he followed that up within the month by bringing in his collection of personal papers and giving them to the History Library. The collection is a treasure. And then he told me some of the stories that he had been involved with at the museum, giving me an institutional history. He was a regent of the Museum of New Mexico. He told me about when he opened the crypt in the cathedral of the Franciscan friars who were being reburied there. He's the one who took out the snippets of the

Figure 10.1 Fray Angélico Chávez, Uncle Sam and His Forty-eight Daughters, *n.d., Collections of the Palace of the Governors (courtesy of the Museum of New Mexico)*

friars' robes and the knotted cord and gave them to his brother, José, who in turn gave them to the museum.[2]

We are fortunate at the museum to have several of his paintings. His cousin, Mónica Sosaya, gave us one he did when he was fifteen, which shows how proud he was to be an American. We talked about how he wasn't accepted by Chicanos. It was because he was proud to be an American who wanted to change the United States to accept what he was and his history. If you asked him about the history he wrote, he would tell you that he was not a revisionist and re-writer. He would say, "I'm a historian, and I'm writing our history within the tenets of history. In a sense, throwing it back in the face of those who compiled the bad history." The painting he did right after New Mexico achieved statehood illustrates this. He was born in 1910 and so was fifteen years old when he painted *Uncle Sam and His Forty-eight Daughters* (fig. 10.1). Each daughter represents a state, the second-to-last of which was New Mexico. The daughters are riding in the car, with Uncle Sam at the wheel. Little houses, cities, and a bay (obviously not New Mexico!) make up the background.

Angélico was a self-taught painter, and one day in 1939 he practiced his art on the inside of a desk drawer. He had recently been ordained and was stationed at Peña Blanca and painted a self-portrait in the drawer (fig. 10.2). He used the back side of the drawer for his palette and signed it "Self-Portrait, Idle

Figure 10.2 Self-portrait, Idle Sketch by Fray Angélico Chávez, *1939, Collections of the Palace of the Governors (courtesy of the Museum of New Mexico)*

Sketch by Fray Angelico Chavez, Peña Blanca, 1939." The portrait was a test for the larger task of painting the Stations of the Cross on the church walls.

Since 1987 I've always been a little bitter about the destruction of the church at Peña Blanca that contained Angélico's magnificent frescoes. The church was torn down under the very authority of the Church that's going to bury him tomorrow. There was a marked change in Fray Angélico when Peña Blanca went down. I think every family member will tell you that. It was as if something in him was broken when the church went down. He did those frescoes when he was twenty-nine years old in a church that was built in the last half of the nineteenth century. He used the townspeople as models.

The church had a structural problem. Water had seeped in back of the nave, and it collapsed. The paintings weren't affected. The church got an appraisal from a company in Albuquerque that we learned later sent a graduate student up to do the job. The estimate was a huge amount to restore the church. I got wind of this. I'm director of probably the oldest adobe building in the state, which has had some major structural problems. In fact, the west wall is leaning out at an angle, and we stabilized that. We have the same water problems that this church had. So I got our architect to meet with certain vicars of the church over lunch to tell them that the estimate they had was wrong. It was too high, and we could get new plans drawn up and an estimate for free and raise the money ourselves to restore the church at Peña Blanca. That's my business, raising money. We got all the dutiful nods, and within weeks after that the church was torn down. One of those vicars was quoted in the papers saying these paintings had no artistic merit.

The Stations of the Cross were spectacular. The people are lifesize. Angélico told me the story that a lady who was blind was led to church by her daughter to be painted, to be used as a model. Who in New Mexico now, since, or ever did frescoes like this? Angélico did the paintings in a year. He talked about putting the wet stucco up and then coloring it and how tedious it was, but he simply did it. Besides painting the interior at Peña Blanca, he also drew on his family, as he was prone to. You've heard about him asking his dad to make the pedestal for La Conquistadora. His father was a carpenter, his mother was a teacher of music in the public schools. His father's best friend was his brother-in-law, Mónica's dad. Everybody in town knew him as Gus Sosaya, and both he and Angélico's dad were carpenters. So Angélico got his Uncle Gus to come down to Peña Blanca and do the doors in front of the church.

Whether the church was destroyed or not, like his mortal body, his works will continue to benefit us all. As we distance ourselves from this week, his reputation will continue to grow. We will learn more of him in the future than we know now—we will learn more than he would want. But, above all, his contributions to art and humanity will loom large. He is probably New Mexico's greatest man of arts and letters.

NOTES

1. See Mason Sutherland, "Adobe New Mexico," *National Geographic* 96 (Dec. 1949), pp. 783–830.

2. In 1957, during the renovation of Saint Francis Cathedral, Fray Angélico opened an

abandoned tomb behind the sanctuary that held the remains of two Franciscan friars who had died in the mid-seventeenth century and had been reburied in the cathedral a century later. He cut a piece of each of the Franciscan habits that had been used to wrap the bones in the reburial and a small section of the knotted cord they had been tied with, in order to preserve the only known examples of the blue habit worn by eighteenth-century Franciscans. He then had the remains moved to a more prominent position in La Conquistadora Chapel. See Fray Angélico Chávez, "The Unique Tomb of Fathers Zárate and De La Llana in Santa Fe," *New Mexico Historical Review* 40 (April 1965), pp. 101–15.

CONTRIBUTORS

MURRAY BODO, O.F.M., is a Franciscan priest. The author of fifteen books, he is at present writer-in-residence at Thomas More College, Crestview Hills, Kentucky. He earned a Ph.D. in literary criticism and composition from the University of Cincinnati in 1992 and has been published in several literary magazines. His best-selling *Francis, the Journey and the Dream* has sold over 160,000 copies and has been translated into seven languages. In 1992 his short story "The Blue Chariot" won the Belly-of-the-Whale Award of *Ambergris Magazine* and was nominated for a Pushcart Prize. Father Murray's latest book is *Tales of an Endishodi: Father Berard Haile and the Navajos, 1900–1961* (University of New Mexico Press, 1998). "After the Earthquakes," a poem about the Assisi earthquakes, has been accepted by *The Paris Review.* At present Fr. Murray is coauthoring with Mark Evan Chimsky a book about religious retreat.

THOMAS E. CHÁVEZ received his Ph.D. in history from the University of New Mexico. He has published four books and numerous articles, including *Manuel Alvarez, 1794–1856: A Southwestern Biography* and *An Illustrated History of New Mexico* (University Press of Colorado, 1990 and 1996). Dr. Chávez is director of the Palace of the Governors at the Museum of New Mexico, Santa Fe. A nephew of Fray Angélico Chávez, he is currently preparing his uncle's last book for publication.

CLARK COLAHAN is associate professor of foreign languages at Whitman College in Walla Walla, Washington, specializing in Renaissance Spanish and colonial New Mexican literatures. His joint translation with Celia Weller of Cervantes's last book, *The Trials of Persiles and Sigismunda,* has been published by University of California Press. He authored *The Visions of Sor María de Agreda* (University of Arizona Press, 1994), about the author of the best-known biography of the Virgin Mary, and helped Spanish national television make a documentary on her legend in New Mexico for the series "Mujeres en la historia."

MARIO T. GARCÍA is professor of history and Chicano studies at the University of California, Santa Barbara. He is the author of numerous works on Chicano history, including *Desert Immigrants: The Mexicans of El Paso, 1880–1920* (Yale University Press, 1981); *Mexican Americans: Leadership, Ideology & Identity, 1930–1960* (Yale University Press, 1989); *Memories of Chicano History: The Life and Narrative of Bert Corona* (University of California Press, 1994); *Ruben Salazar, Border Correspondent: Selected Writings, 1955–1970* (University of California Press, 1995); and *The Making of a Mexican American Mayor: Raymond L. Telles of El Paso* (Texas Western Press, 1998). He is at work on a coauthored biography of Fray Angélico Chávez with Ellen McCracken.

LUIS LEAL is the dean of Mexican American intellectuals in the United States. In his illustrious career, Leal has taught at the University of Mississippi, Emory University, the University of Illinois at Urbana, and the University of California, Santa Barbara, where an endowed chair has been established in his honor. He has published widely on Latin American, Mexican, and Chicano literatures, including 30 books and over 250 articles. Among his most distinguished works are *Breve historia del cuento mexicano* (1956); *Juan Rulfo* (1983); *Mariano Azuela: vida y obra* (1961); and *Aztlán y México: perfiles literarios e históricos* (1985). He has received countless awards, including the Aguila Azteca from Mexico in 1991 and the National Humanities Medal from the United States in 1997.

MANUEL M. MARTÍN-RODRÍGUEZ is associate professor of Latino and Latin American literatures at Texas A & M University. He has published *Rolando Hinojosa y su "cronicón" chicano: Una novela del lector* (Universidad de Sevilla, 1993) and *La voz urgente: Antología de literatura chicana en español* (Madrid: Fundamentos, 1995). His articles have appeared in such journals as *The Americas Review, Hispanic Journal, Hispania, Bilingual Review, Revista Iberoamericana,* and *Latin American Literary Review.*

ELLEN McCRACKEN is professor of Spanish and Portuguese at the University of California, Santa Barbara, where she teaches Latin American literature, U.S. Latino literature, and cultural semiotics. She has written *Decoding Women's Magazines: From* Mademoiselle *to* Ms. (St. Martin's, 1993) and *New Latina Narrative: The Feminine Space of Postmodern Ethnicity* (University of Arizona Press, 1999). She is currently coauthoring a biography of Fray Angélico Chávez with Mario García.

JACK CLARK ROBINSON, O.F.M., is a Franciscan friar and priest, a member of the Province of Our Lady of Guadalupe headquartered in Albuquerque, New Mexico. Since finishing his studies for the priesthood at the Catholic Theological Union in Chicago in 1985, he has spent his time in the pastoral ministry in New Mexico and in the training of those studying to become Franciscans. In addition to his duties as pastor of Holy Family Church in Albuquerque and director of the Franciscan Candidacy Program in Los Lunas, New Mexico, he pursues research and writing on American Franciscan history.

MARC SIMMONS, author and historian, has published thirty books on New Mexico and the Southwest. Among them are *Yesterday in Santa Fe* (Sunstone Press, 1989), *The Last Conquistador* (University of Oklahoma Press, 1991), *Coronado's Land: Essays on Daily Life in Colonial New Mexico* (University of New Mexico Press, 1991) and *The Old Trail to Santa Fe* (University of New Mexico Press, 1996). He has been a Woodrow Wilson and a Guggenheim fellow and was inducted into Spain's Order of Isabela la Católica. He resides on a small ranch near Cerrillos, New Mexico.

THOMAS J. STEELE, S.J., is a Jesuit priest and curator of the five-hundred-piece collection of *santos* (religious folk statues of Hispanic New Mexico) at Regis University, Denver. He is professor emeritus of English at Regis University and adjunct professor of philosophy for religious studies at the University of New Mexico. He spends most of his time researching the religious culture of Hispanic New Mexico. Among his books are *Guidebook to Zen and the Art of Motorcycle Maintenance* (William Morrow, 1990); *Santos and Saints*, 3rd edition (Ancient City Press, 1994); *The Regis Santos* (LPD Press, 1997); and *New Mexico Spanish Religious Oratory* (University of New Mexico Press, 1998). At present he is studying 190 sermons of Archbishop Jean Baptiste Lamy of Santa Fe with the aim of drawing his intellectual and psychological profiles. He wrote the foreword to the reprint of Fray Angélico's *My Penitente Land* (Santa Fe: Museum of New Mexico Press, 1993).

BIBLIOGRAPHY
Books by Fray Angélico Chávez[1]

POETRY AND FICTION

Cantares: Canticles and Poems of Youth, 1925–1932. Detroit: Duns Scotus College, 1932
(bound, typewritten book in the Fray Angélico Chávez History Library, Palace of the
Governors, Santa Fe)

Clothed with the Sun. Santa Fe: Writers' Editions, 1939

Eleven Lady Lyrics and Other Poems. Paterson, N.J.: St. Anthony Guild Press, 1945

From an Altar Screen: El Retablo: Tales From New Mexico. Illustrated by Peter Hurd. New
York: Farrar, Straus & Cudahy. 1957; reprinted Freeport, N.Y.: Books for Libraries
Press, 1969; reprinted under the title *When the Santos Talked: A Retablo of New
Mexican Tales.* Santa Fe: William Gannon, 1977

Guitars and Adobes (under the pseudonym F. Chalmers Ayers). Lithographed by Gerald
Cassidy. Published serially in *St. Anthony Messenger,* 39 (Nov. 1931, 249–252, 268; Dec.
1931, 299–302, 334; Jan. 1932, 346–349, 362; Feb. 1932, 393–397, 401; Mar. 1932, 443–
447, 480; Apr. 1932, 489–491, 504; May 1932, 537–541, 552, 573, 575–576; June 1932,
15–17, 21).

*I—John: A Novela about the Origins and Background of Revelation, or the Apocalypse, Told in
Two Parts: Liaison in Damascus and The Ephesian Connection.* Manuscript in the Fray
Angélico Chávez Collection, Fray Angélico Chávez History Library, Palace of the
Governors, Santa Fe.

New Mexico Triptych, Being Three Panels and Three Accounts: 1. The Angel's New Wings;

1. Updated bibliography based on Phyllis S. Morales, *Fray Angélico Chávez: A Bibliography of His Published Writings, 1925–1978* (Santa Fe: The Lightning Tree: 1980) and documents found in the Fray Angélico Chávez History Library, Santa Fe, New Mexico and the
Franciscan Archives of St. John the Baptist Province, Cincinnati, Ohio. See pages 18–78 of
Morales's thorough bibliography for a list of Chávez's hundreds of articles, poems, fiction,
book reviews, music, plays, and other writings.

2. *The Penitente Thief; 3. Hunchback Madonna.* Illustrated by the author. Paterson,
    N.J.: St. Anthony Guild Press, 1940; second edition with Foreword by Erna
    Fergusson Fresno, Calif.: Academy Guild Press, 1959; reprint of 1940 edition Santa Fe:
    William Gannon, 1976
Selected Poems With an Apologia. Santa Fe: Press of the Territorian, 1969
The Short Stories of Fray Angélico Chávez. Edited by Genaro M. Padilla. Albuquerque:
    University of New Mexico Press, 1987
The Single Rose: The Rosa Única and Commentary of Fray Manuel de Santa Clara. Santa Fe:
    Los Santos Bookshop, 1948
The Song of Francis. Illustrated by Judy Graese. Flagstaff, Ariz.: Northland Press, 1973;
    reprinted London: Sheldon Press, 1978
The Virgin of Port Lligat. Fresno, Calif.: Academy Library Guild, 1959

HISTORICAL AUTOBIOGRAPHY AND NOVEL

La Conquistadora: The Autobiography of an Ancient Statue. Paterson, N.J.: St. Anthony
    Guild Press, 1954; revised edition Santa Fe: Sunstone Press, 1983
The Lady From Toledo. Illustrated by Fray Angélico Chávez. Fresno, Calif.: Academy Guild
    Press, 1969; revised with new notes, historical article, and foreword under the title
    The Lady From Toledo: An Historical Novel in Santa Fe. Santa Fe: Friends-of-The-
    Palace Press, Museum of New Mexico, 1993

HISTORY

Archives of the Archdiocese of Santa Fe, 1678–1900. Washington, D.C.: Academy of
    American Franciscan History, 1957
But Time and Chance: The Story of Padre Martínez of Taos. 1793–1867. Santa Fe: Sunstone
    Press, 1981
Chávez: A Distinctive American Clan of New Mexico. Santa Fe: William Gannon, 1989
Coronado's Friars. Washington, D.C.: Academy of American Franciscan History, 1968
My Penitente Land: Reflections on Spanish New Mexico. Albuquerque: University of New
    Mexico Press, 1974; reprinted Santa Fe: William Gannon, 1979; reprinted with an
    Introduction by Thomas J. Steele, S.J., Santa Fe: Museum of New Mexico Press, 1993
New Mexico Roots Ltd. 11-volume bound manuscript, Special Collections, University of
    New Mexico Library, Albuquerque
*Origins of New Mexico Families in the Spanish Colonial Period. In Two Parts: The Seventeenth
    (1598–1693) and the Eighteenth (1693–1821) Centuries.* With four illustrations by José
    Cisneros. Santa Fe: The Historical Society of New Mexico, 1954; second edition
    Albuquerque: Calvin Horn, 1973; third edition Santa Fe: William Gannon, 1975;
    revised edition, *Origins of New Mexico Families: A Genealogy of the Spanish Colonial
    Period.* With a new Foreword by Thomas E. Chávez. Santa Fe: Museum of New
    Mexico Press, 1992

Our Lady of the Conquest. Santa Fe: The Historical Society of New Mexico, 1948

Très Macho—He Said: Padre Gallegos of Albuquerque, New Mexico's First Congressman. Santa Fe: William Gannon, 1985

TRANSLATIONS

Domínguez, Francisco Atanasio. *Missions of New Mexico, 1776: A Description by Fray Franciso Atanasio Domínguez With Other Contemporary Documents.* Translated and annotated by Eleanor B. Adams and Fray Angélico Chávez. Drawings by Horace T. Pierce. Albuquerque: University of New Mexico Press, 1956; reprinted 1975

Oroz, Pedro. *The Oroz Codex, The Oroz Relación: Or Relation of the Description of the Holy Gospel Province in New Spain and the Lives of the Founders and Other Noteworthy Men of Said Province Composed by Fray Pedro Oroz: 1584–1586.* Translated and edited by Fray Angélico Chávez. Washington D.C.: Academy of American Franciscan History, 1972

Vélez de Escalante, Silvestre. *The Domínguez-Escalante Journal: Their Expedition Through Colorado, Utah, Arizona, and New Mexico in 1776.* Translated by Fray Angélico Chávez and edited by Ted J. Warner. Provo, Utah: Brigham Young University Press, 1976

MONOGRAPHS

The Cathedral of the Royal City of the Holy Faith of St. Francis. Santa Fe: Schiffani Bros., 1947; revised editions under the title *The Santa Fe Cathedral* 1968, 1978, 1987, and 1995

Lamy Memorial. Santa Fe: Schiffani Bros., 1951

The Lord and New Mexico. Albuquerque: Archdiocese of Santa Fe, 1975

The Old Faith and Old Glory: Story of the Church in New Mexico Since the American Occupation, 1846–1946. Santa Fe: Archdiocese of Santa Fe, 1946

MEDITATION

Seraphic Days: Franciscan Thoughts and Affections on the Principal Feasts of Our Lord and Our Lady and All the Saints of the Three Orders of the Seraph of Assisi. Edited by Father Sebastian Erbacher, O.F.M. Paterson, N.J.: St. Anthony Guild, 1940

El Via Crucis de San Leonardo. Cincinnati: St. Anthony Messenger Press, 1947

INDEX